LLC Operating Agreements Line by Line

A Detailed Look at LLC Operating Agreements and How to Draft Them to Meet Your Clients' Needs

Frank A. Ciatto and Joseph B. Walker Jr.

ASPATORE

ISBN 9780314288097

Mat #41458717

ASPATORE

Aspatore Books, a Thomson Reuters business, exclusively publishes C-Level executives and partners from the world's most respected companies and law firms. Each publication provides professionals of all levels with proven business and legal intelligence from industry insiders—direct and unfiltered insight from those who know it best. Aspatore Books is committed to publishing an innovative line of business and legal titles that lay forth principles and offer insights that can have a direct financial impact on the reader's business objectives.

ACKNOWLEDGMENT

Joe and I would both like to acknowledge the mentoring and tutelage provided over the years by Venable Senior Partner Stef Tucker. Without Stef's fine lawyering, this book would not have been possible.

—Frank Ciatto

DEDICATION

To my wife, Deanne, and our three terrific daughters, Sophia, Francesca and Julianna, who all make the hard work worth it each and every day.

—Frank Ciatto

To Jen, Rebecca, Julianne, Emily, Dallin, Tommy and Sarah, for your unwavering support, encouragement, patience and understanding.

—Joseph B. Walker Jr.

CONTENTS

Introduction

The beginning of a new business often begins with the formation of a legal entity out of which the business will be operated. Given the flexible governance structure and favorable pass-through tax treatment, limited liability companies (LLCs) have become the entity of choice for most new small businesses.

Formation of an LLC generally involves little more than filing a one-page document with a given state and paying a nominal filing fee. Because states do not require the members of an LLC to enter into an operating agreement, members may be tempted to skip this step or resort to generic, inadequate documents not tailored to their specific needs. However, almost without fail, this leads to issues down the road. When issues arise and there is either no operating agreement, or an inadequate operating agreement is in place, the parties are forced to resolve their disputes through tense and lengthy negotiations or even expensive and uncertain litigation. Experience has repeatedly demonstrated that careful attention to the preparation of the operating agreement will result in benefits to the members as the business operations intensify and unexpected challenges and successes are encountered.

Operating agreements define the relationship among the business owners and the procedures for the management and operation of the LLC. They are drafted to resolve issues such as:

- How much money each party is required to contribute to the LLC now, and in the future.
- How important decisions will be made. How deadlocks will be resolved.
- What happens if one of the owners dies or is unable to continue participating in the business.
- Whether the owners can sell their interest in the business to third parties.
- What happens if one owner wants to buy out the other owner(s).
- What happens if business partners wish to separate.
- Whether the owners are permitted to start competing or similar businesses.
- Whether one owner can force the other to sell to a third-party acquirer.
- How profits will be distributed. Who decides how much to distribute.

These and other issues take on increased importance when businesses or their owners face difficult circumstances not envisioned when the business was first formed. Unfortunately, some members find themselves trying to sort through these difficult and emotionally charged questions at the worst possible time, instead of addressing them before the business commences.

Several key areas of discussion and negotiation must be resolved in every operating agreement. The attached operating agreement (the agreement) is intended to demonstrate the most typical resolution of these issues. A brief summary of some of the most substantive terms and conditions addressed in an operating agreement, as well as the manner in which the attached agreement addresses such issues is set forth below:

Capital Contributions

(1) Initial Contributions: The agreement reflects that each member has contributed or caused to be contributed to the company their respective shares of the company's initial assets.

(2) Future Contributions: If the manager determines that the company requires additional funds for the operation of its business, the manager may cause the company to borrow such funds from commercial banks, savings and loan associations, and/or other lending institutions or from any other persons, including any member or affiliates thereof. If the manager does not cause the company to borrow the funds needed, the members may make additional capital contributions to the company. If members do not make capital contributions in proportion to their respective percentage interests, the interests of those making larger contributions will be increased and the interests of those making smaller contributions will be diluted.

Allocation of Profit and Loss

Profits and losses of the company are allocated proportionately among the members in accordance with their respective percentage ownership interests in the company, as reflected in Exhibit A to the agreement.

Distributions

(1) Distributions of Net Cash Flow: Distributions of net cash flow of the company are to be distributed to the members in accordance with their

respective percentage interests not less frequently than annually, at the times and in the aggregate amounts determined by the manager. Net cash flow includes total cash receipts of the company, plus any other funds deemed available for distribution as net cash flow by the manager, in the manager's reasonable discretion, less total cash disbursements of the company, and less any reserves or other uses of cash deemed reasonably necessary as the manager shall determine.

(2) Distributions upon Dissolution: Upon the dissolution of the company, the net proceeds from the sale or liquidation of the assets of the company, as well as any other non-liquidated assets of the company, will be distributed: (i) first, to the creditors of the company in order to satisfy any and all of the outstanding company debts; (ii) second, to the members of the company, *pro rata*, in accordance with their respective positive capital account balances; and (iii) finally, to the members of the company, *pro rata*, in proportion to their respective percentage interests.

Management

(1) Designation of Managers; Authority: The company will be managed by the manager (or managers). Class A members maintain the right to appoint and replace the manager(s). Class B members have no voting rights.

(2) Tax Matters Partners: The tax matters partner will correspond directly with the Internal Revenue Service in the event of an audit of the company's income tax return or as to any information requested by the IRS.

Indemnification of Manager

The agreement provides for the indemnification of the manager for actions taken on behalf of the company.

Assignment of Interest

(1) Transfer Other than by Sale: No member may assign, transfer, or pledge his or her legal membership interest in the company without the prior written consent of the manager. Notwithstanding the foregoing, any member may transfer his or her membership interest to a "permitted transferee," which includes (i) a descendant or descendants of such member, (ii) any person already a member, (iii) a beneficiary of any trust that is a member, or (iv) a trust, whether *inter vivos* or

testamentary, in which any person or entity named in (i), (ii) or (iii) above is a primary income beneficiary.

(2) Sale of Interest: If a member desires to sell his or her entire membership interest in the company to a third party, such member must first obtain a "bona fide offer" (that is, an offer from an unaffiliated third party) to purchase such member's interest in the company. In such event, the other members will have the right to purchase the selling member's interest in accordance with the terms of the bona fide offer. If the other members do not wish to purchase such member's interest in the company, the selling member will have the right to sell such interest in accordance with the terms of the bona fide offer.

Resignation or Withdrawal of a Member

No member may voluntarily resign or withdraw from the company and demand the return of his or her capital account prior to the dissolution and termination of the company.

Death, Insanity, Incompetency, or Termination of a Member

In the event of the death, insanity, incompetency, or termination of a member that is a trust or other entity, the estate or other legal representative of the withdrawing member shall have the right to transfer such withdrawing member's interest in the company to such withdrawing member's heirs, beneficiaries, distributes, or other successor parties. Such transferees will have the same rights and obligations as that of the withdrawing member but shall not be considered a substituted member until admitted into the company pursuant to the agreement. As an alternative to this standard provision, we sometimes include a provision in which living members have the right to buy out the deceased member's interest for the fair market value of such interest.

Bankruptcy of a Member

In the event of the bankruptcy of any member, the other members will have the option (but not the obligation) to purchase the membership interest owned by the bankrupt member for an amount equal to the fair market value of such membership interest. The fair market value of the bankrupt member's interest may be determined by the legal representative of the bankrupt member and the other members who elect to exercise the option; however, if there is no agreement between such parties, then the fair market value of the bankrupt member's interest will be determined by a three-appraiser procedure.

Dissolution

The company will be dissolved and liquidated upon (i) the unanimous consent of the managers and the members; (ii) at any time the company has no members for a period of ninety consecutive days; (iii) the entry of a decree of judicial dissolution under the act; or (iv) the occurrence of any other event causing the dissolution of a limited liability company under the laws of the state of Delaware.

Line-by-Line Analysis

LIMITED LIABILITY COMPANY AGREEMENT
OF
NEWCO, LLC

July 1, 2012

LIMITED LIABILITY COMPANY AGREEMENT
OF
NEWCO, LLC

THIS LIMITED LIABILITY COMPANY AGREE-MENT is made and entered into, effective for all purposes and in all respects as of the 1st day of July, 2012, by and among the undersigned parties.

This form agreement is intended as an illustration of current best practices for newly formed, privately held limited liability companies as of July 1, 2012, the date of formation for the fictional "NEWCO, LLC."

WHEREAS, certain undersigned parties have formed (or caused to be formed) a limited liability company known as "Newco, LLC" (the "Company," as defined herein), for the purposes set forth in Article IV hereof, pursuant to the "Act" (as defined herein) and other relevant laws of the State of Delaware; and

WHEREAS, the undersigned parties desire to set forth herein their agreements and understandings with respect to the ownership and operation of the Company.

The recitals to the LLC agreement are generally generic in the first iteration of the agreement. When the agreement is amended and restated, more detailed recitals are appropriate to describe the genesis of the LLC agreement, the admission of new members, the transfer of membership interests, major transactions giving rise to the amendment and restatement, or the ongoing business operations of the LLC.

NOW, THEREFORE, in consideration of the foregoing and other good and valuable consideration, the receipt and sufficiency of which are hereby acknowledged, the undersigned parties, intending legally and equitably to be bound, hereby covenant and agree as follows:

ARTICLE I

Definitions

Not every definition will be addressed in detail. Those definitions that do not require further explanation, as well as those that will be discussed in other sections of this document will not be addressed in Article I.

1. **The following terms shall have the indicated meanings ascribed to them when used herein:**

   "Act" shall mean and refer to the Delaware Limited Liability Company Act [Delaware Code Annotated, Title 6, §§18-101 *et seq.* (1992)].

   "Additional Capital Contributions" shall mean and refer to any additional cash Capital Contributions made by a Member to the Company in order to fund any Additional Funds under Article VI-2 hereof, *reduced by* distributions to such Member pursuant to Article XII-1 hereof.

   "Additional Funds" shall have the meaning ascribed to such term in Article VI-2 hereof.

   "Affiliate" shall mean, as to any Person, any other Person controlled by, controlling or under common control with such Person, and "control" means the power to manage or direct the affairs of the Person in question, whether by ownership of voting securities, by contract, or otherwise.

The concept of "affiliates" is applicable throughout the agreement to address the permissible interplay between the company and other entities and/or persons that are related to, or controlled by the members. The "affiliates" definition generally seeks to capture individuals who are directly related to a member, as well as those entities that are owned or operated by any of the members. The use of the "affiliates" concept throughout the agreement can be permissive to permit membership interest transfers to, and/or coordinated business activities with affiliates, or it can be restrictive in an attempt to limit or prohibit interactions between the company and other entities owned by the members. With respect to entities that are included as affiliates, this definition is intended to capture those entities that are "controlled" by a member, however, the scope of affiliates can be extended to include all entities in which a member holds (directly or indirectly) a certain percentage ownership interest, even if such entity is not "controlled" by the member.

"Agreement" shall mean and refer to this Limited Liability Company Agreement and Exhibit A attached hereto, as originally executed and as amended from time to time in writing.

"Bankruptcy" (and any derivations thereof) shall mean and refer to an adjudication of bankruptcy under Title 11 of the United States Code, as amended, an assignment for the benefit of creditors and/or an adjudication of insolvency under any state or local insolvency statute or procedure or the occurrence of any other event of bankruptcy or insolvency under the Act.

"Capital Account" shall, with respect to each Member, mean and refer to the separate "book" account for such Member to be established and maintained in all events in the manner provided under, and in accordance with, Treasury Regulation §1.704-1(b)(2)(iv), as amended, and in accordance with the other provisions of Treasury Regulation §1.704-1(b) that must be complied with in order for the Capital Accounts to be determined and maintained in accordance with the provisions of Treasury Regulation §1.704-1(b)(2)(iv). In furtherance of and consistent with the foregoing, a Member's Capital Account shall include generally, without limitation, the Capital Contributions of such Member (as of any particular date), (i) increased by such

Member's distributive share of Profit of the Company (including, if such date is not the close of the Company Accounting Year, the distributive share of Profit of the Company for the period from the close of the last Company Accounting Year to such date), and (ii) decreased by such Member's distributive share of Loss of the Company and distributions by the Company to such Member (including, if such date is not the close of the Company Accounting Year, the distributive share of Loss of the Company and distributions by the Company during the period from the close of the last Company Accounting Year to such date). For purposes of the foregoing, distributions of property shall result in a decrease in a Member's Capital Account equal to the agreed fair market value of such property distributed (less the amount of indebtedness, if any, of the Company which is assumed by such Member and/or the amount of indebtedness, if any, to which such property is subject, as of the date of distribution) by the Company to such Member.

"Capital Contribution" or "Capital Contributions" shall mean and refer to the amount of cash and/or the agreed fair market value of property [less the amount of indebtedness, if any, of a Member which is assumed by the Company and/or the amount of indebtedness, if any, to which such property is subject, as of the date of contribution (without regard to the provisions of I.R.C. Section 7701(g))] actually contributed by a Member to the capital of the Company, including, but not limited to, any amounts paid by a Member (except to the extent indemnification is made by another Member) in respect of any claims, liabilities or obligations against the Company and/or pursuant to any guaranty of Company indebtedness or otherwise by such Member.

"Certificate" shall mean and refer to that certain Certificate of Formation of the Company filed with, and approved by, the Office of the Secretary of State of Delaware, as the same may be amended, modified, supplemented and/or restated from time to time.

"Class A Member" or "Class A Members" shall mean and refer to that Person or those Persons designated as such in Exhibit A.

The membership of NEWCO consists of both Class A and Class B members. Class A members are the founding members of NEWCO who have contributed capital and have both voting and economic interests in NEWCO. The Class B membership interests are non-voting profits interests with a prospective interest in only the annual profits of NEWCO as well as a portion of the growth in the value of the company after the date on which the Class B membership interest is granted. Generally, the Class B membership interests are offered as incentive compensation to key employees of the company to give them an ongoing interest in the financial performance and economic growth of the company.

"Class A Membership Units" shall mean and refer to Membership Units granted or assigned to a Class A Member or Class A Members.

"Class B Member" or "Class B Members" shall mean and refer to that Person or those Persons designated as such in Exhibit A.

"Class B Membership Units" shall mean and refer to Membership Units granted to a Class B Member or Class B Members.

"Company" shall mean and refer to Newco, LLC, a Delaware limited liability company formed under and pursuant to the Act and other relevant laws of the State of Delaware and owned and operated pursuant to the terms of this Agreement.

"Company Accounting Year" shall mean and refer to the twelve (12)-month period ending December 31 of

> **each year, which shall constitute the accounting year of the Company, or any shorter period applicable hereunder.**

The company accounting year can be either a fiscal or calendar year, depending on the choice of the members, and whether the company adopts cash or accrual accounting methods. Regardless of which twelve-month period is chosen as the company accounting year, the managers should note the interplay between the accounting periods chosen by the company and the deadlines for the tax liabilities of the members of the company. This is particularly apparent in instances where the company operates on a non-calendar accounting year, the individual members are nevertheless required to file their taxes on a calendar year basis.

> **"Company Assets" at any particular time, shall mean and refer to all property and assets (tangible or intangible, choate or inchoate, fixed or contingent) which the Company may own, hold, acquire, operate and/or manage from time to time, as such assets are more fully described on the books and records of the Company.**

> **"Company Interest," as to any Member, shall mean and refer to the entire ownership interest of such Member in the Company at any particular time, including such Member's Capital Account, Membership Units, right to distributions under Article XII-1 hereof and the right of such Member to any and all benefits to which a Member may be entitled as provided in this Agreement and under the Act, together with the obligations of such Member to comply with all of the terms and provisions of this Agreement and the Act.**

The company interest of a member is an all-inclusive concept of each member's total ownership interest in the company and includes each member's ability to participate in the economic performance of the company. "Company interest" contrasts with the concept of "percentage interest," which analyzes each member's participation rights in comparison the participation rights of the other members. In other LLC agreements, this term can be referred to as an "interest" (which we find to be confusing) or a "membership interest."

> **"Competing Business" shall mean and refer to (1) any business that is similar or related to the business of the Company, or (2) the rendering of services that are the same or substantially the same as the services, if any, rendered by such Member on behalf of the Company.**

Non-compete agreements within an operating agreement can be a contentious but necessary provision. If some or all of the members will not be employed full-time by the company, they may be unwilling to agree to a restrictive covenant that will severely inhibit their ability to participate in other existing or new ventures or business opportunities. Conversely, a silent investor member may wish to limit the ability of the "sweat equity" members to take the knowledge and experience developed in their work for the company and use it to compete against the company in a later business. Properly defining what constitutes a "competing business" establishes the appropriate boundaries that permit reasonable participation in similar or related businesses by the members, without permitting a member to use the resources and/or knowledge of the company to create a competitor.

> **"Exhibit A" shall mean and refer to the original Exhibit A to this Agreement, relating to the names and addresses of the Class A Members and the Class B Members, as may be amended from time to time.**

> **"Fair Market Value" of a Company Interest shall be determined based on the price which would be paid by a willing buyer to a willing seller in an arms'-length transaction for the purchase of such Company Interest, free and clear of any option, call, contract, commitment, demand, lien, charge, security interest or encumbrance of any kind whatsoever, as such price may be mutually determined by the interested Members (or groups of interested Members) and the**

Company (as applicable), or, if the interested
Members (or groups of interested Members) and the
Company (as applicable) cannot mutually agree upon
such price within fifteen (15) days after the event
triggering a determination of Fair Market Value, the
Fair Market Value of such Company Interest shall be
determined as follows: The interested parties shall
agree on a single appraiser within thirty (30) days
after the expiration of the fifteen (15)-day period
above or, if the interested parties are unable to agree
on a single appraiser, then each interested Member
(or group of interested Members) and the Company
(as applicable) shall promptly appoint an appraiser,
who or which shall determine mutually the Fair
Market Value of such Company Interest, for purposes
of an all-cash sale. All appraisers appointed hereunder
shall be directed to take into account any "minority
ownership discounts," "lack of marketability
discounts" and/or other applicable valuation discounts
in valuing such Company Interest.

Proper calculation of applicable discounts is a significant issue when
determining the fair market value of an LLC membership interest. The fact
that most LLCs are closely held and not publicly traded materially decreases
both (i) the value of units that do not control the LLC, and (ii) the ability of
members to liquidate their units for cash. Thus, in an open market, a minority
interest in an LLC would be worth less than its *pro rata* portion of the total
value of the LLC. This fact should be taken into account when valuing the
company interests.

If the two (2) appraisers agree upon the fair market
value of the Company Interest, they shall jointly render
a single written report of their opinion thereon;
provided, however, that, if the two (2) appraisers cannot
agree upon the fair market value of the Company
Interest and their respective appraisals are within ten
percent (10%) of each other, then the Fair Market Value
shall be the average of the two (2) appraisals; and

> provided, further that if the two (2) appraisers cannot agree upon the fair market value of the Company Interest and their respective appraisals are not within ten percent (10%) of each other, then they shall together appoint a third (3rd) appraiser, who or which shall determine the Fair Market Value of such Company Interest, and shall send written notice of such determination to each Member.

The method adopted in the operating agreement is not nearly as important as having a detailed, *ex ante* agreement as to how fair market value will be determined. Having said that, we prefer the so-called "baseball method" because, although it can be costly, it offers a "checks and balances" approach to a scenario that often times pits an LLC insider (i.e., the company and its living members) against an outsider (i.e., the executor of the estate of a deceased member). When adopting a method that employs an appraiser, the members will want to consider carefully what information the appraiser should take into account including applicable discounts such as minority or lack of marketability, or other relevant information that will affect the true value of the company interest at issue.

> All appraisers appointed shall be duly licensed and qualified by experience and ability to value entities similar to the Company; and the fees and other costs of each of the first two (2) appraisers shall be borne by the Member (or group of Members) or the Company (as applicable) appointing each such appraiser, with the fees and other costs of the third (3rd) appraiser (if applicable) being shared equally by the Company and the Members (or group of Members). The Fair Market Value determined by the first two (2) appraisers or the third (3rd) appraiser (as the case may be) shall be used to determine the purchase price of the Company Interest; provided, however, that, if the Fair Market Value determined by the third (3rd) appraiser is more than the higher of the first two (2) appraisers, the higher determination of the first two (2) appraisers shall govern; and provided, further, that if the Fair

> **Market Value determined by the third (3rd) appraiser**
> **is less than the lower determination of the first two (2)**
> **appraisers, the lower determination of the first two (2)**
> **appraisers shall govern.**

The "fair market value" concept has a significant effect in the operating agreement, most notably, in determining the price at which company interests are purchased as members either choose or are required to relinquish their company interests. There are a number of methods from which the members can pick to determine fair market value; this agreement adopts the "baseball method" wherein the interested members agree on an appraiser or, if no agreement can be reached, then each interested member picks an appraiser and those appraisers jointly appoint the appraiser who will determine the fair market value.

> **"Indemnified Party" shall have the meaning ascribed**
> **to such term in Article X-9(a) hereof.**

> **"I.R.C." shall mean and refer to the Internal Revenue**
> **Code of 1986, as amended, or any similar Federal**
> **internal revenue law enacted in substitution of the**
> **Internal Revenue Code of 1986, and the corresponding**
> **revenue law (and sections thereof) of any state or**
> **jurisdiction.**

> **"Loss" shall have the meaning ascribed to such term**
> **in Article VII-1 hereof.**

> **"Manager" or "Managers" shall mean and refer**
> **initially to [_____], and [_____], subject to the**
> **provisions of Article X-2 hereof.**

This agreement contemplates one or more managers of the company, however, the management control of the company can be tailored to meet the particular needs of the members and the company. Management structures can be as simple as a member-managed LLC, and as complex as a board of managers and company officers, if necessary.

> **"Member" or "Members"** shall mean and refer to the Class A Members and the Class B Members designated as such in Exhibit A.

> **"Membership Unit"** and **"Membership Units"** shall mean and refer to the One Hundred (100) Membership Units of membership interest in the Company which the Company is authorized to issue. Each Membership Unit shall represent an undivided membership interest as a Member in the Company.

Introducing the concept of "units" into an LLC is generally not necessary when there is only one class of Members. As Newco will have Class B member employees who will have a profits interest in the company, expressing the company onterests of Class B members as "units" allows the Class A members to limit the disclosure of their respective percentage interests to broad groups of Class B members.

> **"Net Capital Investment"** shall, with respect to each Member, mean and refer to the cash Capital Contributions by such Member to the Company, excluding any Additional Capital Contributions by such Member, *reduced by* any distributions to such Member pursuant to Article XII-1 hereof.

In this agreement, each Class A member has a priority, with respect to Class B members, in the amount of the "net capital investment" of such Class A member. This priority is manifested in the preferred return to which each Class A member is entitled before any distributions of profits are made to Class B members, as well as any distributions that are made to the members in a liquidation scenario. The net capital investment of each member is intended to reflect the actual cash investment amount of each member, therefore, the amount of the net capital investment of each Class B member is zero.

> **"Net Cash Flow"** shall mean and refer to the total cash receipts of the Company (including, without limitation, any loan proceeds, gross sales proceeds and operating revenues, but excluding Capital Contributions), *plus* any

other funds (including amounts previously set aside as reserves by the Managers, where and to the extent the Managers no longer regard such reserves as reasonably necessary in the efficient conduct and/or expansion of the Company business) deemed available for distribution and designated as "Net Cash Flow" by the Managers, in their sole discretion, *less* the total cash disbursements of the Company such as, but not limited to, the salaries and other compensation paid to any employees of the Company, other operating expenses of the Company and repayments of any loans made to the Company by any Person whatsoever (including loans from any Member and/or any Affiliate thereof), *less* such reserves or other uses of cash as the Managers, in their sole discretion, shall deem to be necessary for the efficient conduct of the Company business, including the purchase of additional Company Assets.

The obligation of the company to make distributions to the members is based largely on the extent to which the company has a positive net cash flow. The formulation of net cash flow is intended to capture the actual cash flow of the company that is available to distribute to members after all costs, expenses and liabilities of the company have been accounted for. The net cash flow definition is also intended to account for the reasonable reserves determined by the managers to be necessary for the continued business operations of the company and this language is intended to be broad so that if the managers determine it is reasonably necessary, they may reserve all net cash flow, in a company accounting year, subject to the managers' obligation to distribute net cash flow to cover each member's tax liability.

"Officer" or "Officers" shall mean and refer to that person or those persons appointed by the Managers to serve as (an) executive officer(s) of the Company, which person or persons shall have the right, power and authority to manage and oversee the day-to-day business and operations of the Company, as more fully set forth in Article X-2 hereof.

> **"Percentage Interest"** of a Member shall mean and refer to the percentage participation in the Company of such Member.

Membership interests in a limited liability company incorporate both economic and governance rights in the company. The percentage interest of a member refers to such member's ability to participate in governance and management of the company (in the case of Class A members), and can be different than such member's profit and/or distribution allocation percentage.

> **"Permitted Transferee"** of a Member shall mean and refer to any of the following: (i) such Member's spouse or natural or adopted descendant or descendants, (ii) any Person already a Member, (iii) a trust, whether *inter vivos* or testamentary, in which any person or entity named in (i) or (ii) above is the primary income beneficiary, (iv) a family limited partnership or family limited liability company formed by a Member, in which the sole partners or members (as the case may be) are such Member and/or his Affiliates, or (v) in the case of a Member which is a trust, to any beneficiaries of such trust.

As in most operating agreements, the transfer of membership interests by the members of the company is restricted. In this agreement, the restrictions on transfer do not apply to transfers by a member to a permitted transferee. Generally, the permitted transferees are those individuals and entities to which a member may transfer a membership interest in connection with estate planning strategies (i.e., certain trusts, descendants, and spouses). The concept may be expanded, however, to include any other transferees for which the members agree to permit unrestricted transfers.

> **"Person"** shall mean and refer to an individual or entity, such as, but not limited to, a corporation, general partnership, joint venture, limited partnership, limited liability company, trust, foundation or business association.

"Preferred Return" shall, with respect to any Class A Member, mean and refer to an aggregate amount equal to (i) a twelve percent (12%) *per annum*, cumulative but noncompounded, on such Class A Member's respective Net Capital Investment, as computed and aggregated on a *per diem* basis for each Company Accounting Year comments as of the date such Class A Member makes (or is deemed to have made) Capital Contributions to the Company, *less* (ii) any distributions actually made to such Class A Member under Article XII-2(a) hereof.

The preferred return to which the Class A members are entitled is intended to facilitate a return on the Class A members' cash contributions, and takes precedence over any other distributions of net cash flow to which the Class A or Class B members are entitled. Any due and unpaid preferred return owed to the Class A members takes priority over any other member distributions.

"Prime Rate" shall mean and refer to the "prime rate" offered by U.S. banks as published from time to time in the "Money Rates" section of *The Wall Street Journal*.

"Profit" shall have the meaning ascribed to such term in Article VII-1 hereof.

"Proprietary Information" shall mean any confidential, proprietary and/or trade secret information concerning the Company's products, technology, services, finances, personnel or business methods, practices or policies, including, without limitation, information relating to research and development, know-how, inventions, specifications, software, market analysis, research strategies, projections and forecasts, except to the extent to which a Member can establish by legally sufficient evidence that such information: (i) was rightfully in such Member's possession before receipt from the Company; (ii) is or becomes a matter of public knowledge through no fault of such Member; (iii) is rightfully received by such Member from a third party without violation of any duty of confidentiality; or (iv) is or was independently developed by or for such Member. Subject to the foregoing exceptions, "Proprietary Information" also includes, without limitation, (x) information of a similar nature received by the Company from third parties that the Company is obligated to treat as confidential, and information in combination with publicly known information where the nature of the combination is not publicly known and (y) the same or similar type of information of any Affiliate, regardless of whether the Company transfers this Agreement to any such Affiliate. However, "Proprietary Information" shall not include information regarding a product, service or technology that the Company has determined, in writing, that it will not pursue for commercial exploitation.

The "proprietary information" definition in this agreement is a broad provision to encompass any valuable company information that should be protected by the restrictive covenants in the agreement. The agreement provides that the members may not make use of proprietary information of the company both while they are members of the company and thereafter. A "proprietary information" definition that is general and broad in scope may provide adequate protection for many companies, however, for companies that derive a significant amount of value from intellectual property and trade secrets, it may be beneficial to add specific references to such intellectual property to increase the likelihood that the use of such information will be protected by the restrictive covenants in the agreement.

"Substituted Member" or "Substituted Members" shall mean and refer to that Person or those Persons admitted to the Company as a Member or Members, in accordance with the provisions of Article XIII hereof and so reflected in Exhibit A attached hereto.

"Tax Liability" shall, with respect to each Member, mean an amount equal to the Federal and state income tax liability attributable to any income or gain allocated to such Member by the Company. The Tax Liability shall be equal to the maximum Federal and state income tax rates (based on the state with the highest income tax rate among all the states where the Members reside) that apply to ordinary income or long-term capital gain, as applicable; it being understood and agreed that the Managers may, in their reasonable discretion, take into account Losses from prior Company Accounting Years attributable to a Member and not used by such Member due to at-risk limitations under I.R.C. Section 105 in determining the amount of a Member's Tax Liability to be distributed to a Member.

This agreement provides that the company is required to make cash distributions to the members each year in amounts equal to the expected tax liability to be recognized by each member. Given the pass-through nature of limited liability companies, if tax distributions were not made by the company, the members could incur tax liabilities for their respective *pro rata* share of income of the company, without accompanying cash distributions with which to pay such liabilities. The "tax liability" definition is intended to capture the actual expected tax liability of the members, without creating a distribution obligation for the company if there is no company income to make a distribution.

"Tax Matters Partner" shall have the meaning ascribed to such term in Article X-6(a) hereof.

2. Unless the context clearly indicates otherwise, where appropriate the singular shall include the plural and any pronoun shall include the masculine, feminine and neuter, to the extent necessary to give the terms defined in this Article I and/or the terms otherwise used in this Agreement their proper meanings.

3. Unless specifically and expressly limited in the context, any reference herein to a decision,

determination, act, action, exercise of a right, power or privilege, or other procedure by the Managers shall mean and refer to such decision, determination, act, action, exercise or other procedure of the Managers, in their reasonable discretion.

Under Delaware law, the managers of Newco at a minimum owe the implied duty of good faith and fair dealing to the members. The fiduciary duties of care and loyalty may be expressly adopted, disclosed, or modified in an LLC agreement. In fulfilling their fiduciary obligations (if adopted), the managers are protected by the business judgment rule, which provides a rebuttable presumption that the managers have acted reasonably and in the best interests of the members. Other fiduciary duties can be incorporated or disclaimed under the terms of the LLC agreement, including fiduciary obligations among the members. A comprehensive discussion of fiduciary obligations in LLCs is beyond the scope of this book, however, we note that the proposed restriction or elimination of fiduciary duties should be undertaken only after a careful examination of the underlying motives for such reductions, and the accompanying potential outcomes to the members. See further discussion on fiduciary duties in Article X (8).

ARTICLE II

Name of Company

The name of the Company shall be "Newco, LLC."

ARTICLE III

Term of Company; Formation

A limited liability company agreement and/or certificate of formation can provide for a limited or unlimited term of existence for the company. Generally, companies elect a perpetual term of existence, although there are circumstances where a limited term is appropriate and the members may seek to set a time certain for the dissolution of the limited liability company. For the overwhelming majority of companies, however, it is more appropriate to initially elect a perpetual term, and provide a clear path to dissolution in the LLC agreement.

1. **The Company shall have perpetual existence, unless sooner terminated in accordance with the provisions of Article XV hereof.**

2. **The undersigned Members heretofore authorized [Law Firm] to act as organizer in order to form the Company under and pursuant to the Act by filing the Certificate on behalf of themselves and any additional or Substituted Members. This Agreement is subject to, and governed by, the Act. In the event of a direct conflict between the provisions of this Agreement and the mandatory provisions of the Act, such mandatory provisions of the Act shall be controlling. The Company shall have perpetual existence, unless sooner terminated in accordance with the provisions of Article XV.**

ARTICLE IV

Business of Company

The general purposes and business objectives of the Company are to [_____].

The purposes of an LLC will be determined by the facts and circumstances related to the intended operations of the company and should provide a high-level, general statement of the business objectives of the company. Importantly, the description must include sufficient flexibility to permit the company to grow and expand into related lines of business without requiring amendment to the limited liability company agreement. A narrow description of the operations of the company could prove to be unnecessarily restrictive as the company matures. Note also that the description of the purpose and business objectives of the company serves as a significant reference point in determining what is a "competing business" for purposes of the non-compete covenants.

ARTICLE V

Principal Office; Registered Office and Registered Agent

The principal office of the Company shall be located at [_____]. The Managers may change the principal office of the Company and/or establish additional offices of the Company, either within or without the State of Delaware, as the Managers may deem advisable. The registered office of the Company shall be located at [_____]. The registered agent of the Company in the State of Delaware for service of process shall be [_____], which is a Delaware corporation. The Managers may, in their sole and absolute discretion, change the registered agent of the Company to a Person who or which qualifies as a registered agent under the Act.

ARTICLE VI

Capital Contributions; Membership Units

1. (a) The Company shall issue to each of the Class A Members a number of Membership Units proportionate to each Class A Member's respective Capital Contribution. The Class A Members (in their capacity as Class A Members), have committed to make an aggregate Capital Contribution to the Company, as indicated on Exhibit A, attached hereto.

The Class A membership units issued to the Class A members will be issued in exchange for the initial capital contributions of the Class A members. The initial capital contributions can be nominal or significant contributions, depending on the amounts agreed among the Class A members. The key issue for initial issuances is determining that each member has contributed equivalent value for equivalent issuances of membership units.

(b) (i) None of the Class B Members shall be required to make any Capital Contribution to the Company. Simultaneously with the execution of this Agreement, the Company shall issue to each Class B Member the number of Membership Units set forth in a separate letter to each of the Class B Members.

(ii) Notwithstanding anything to the contrary contained herein, the Company Interest granted to each of the Class B Members is a "profits interest" pursuant to, and in accordance with, Rev. Proc. 93-27 (1992-2 CB 343) and Rev. Proc. 2001-43 (2001-34 IRB 191) (the "Revenue Procedures"). Such Company Interest has been granted to each of the Class B Members in exchange for the provision of services by each such Class B Member for, and on behalf of, the Company. Moreover, the Class B Members' Company Interests granted hereby do not entitle the Class B Members as of the date hereof to a share of the proceeds if the Company Assets were sold at Fair Market Value and such proceeds were distributed in complete liquidation of the Company. Each of the Class B Members hereby agrees to take into account the distributive share of partnership income, gain, loss, deduction and credit associated with such Company Interests in computing his, her or its income tax liability for the entire period during which such Class B Member owns his, her or its Company Interest.

The Class B membership units do not entitle the Class B members to a portion of the company's assets *on the day such Class B units are issued*. The provisions of (b)(i) and (ii) of this section are intended to clarify that Class B membership units provide an interest in the prospective profits and growth in value of the company (both annual profits and sale proceeds), not the current and accumulated assets and profits existing on the date of the issuance. Accordingly, if Newco were to dissolve the day after the issuance of Class B units, such Class B units would have no claim to any assets of Newco. To ensure the proper grant of any Class B membership units, such grant should be made only after an independent third-party appraisal of the company, which will create a baseline value of the company that such a Class B member would not share.

> **(iii) In accordance with the Revenue Procedures, the grant of the Company Interest to the Class B Members hereby is not a taxable event.**

The Class B units are intended to be issued as incentive compensation to employees of the company. As such, Class B members do not have voting rights, and the Class B members have no claim to the assets or accumulated profits of the company. As the Class B units have no value on the day of issuance, there is no income to the employees upon receipt of the Class B units, and no recognition of taxable income. It is important to note, however, that Class B members will recognize future taxable income in the amount of their respective *pro rata* share of any future profits and growth in value of the company. As the Class B members are often less experienced in such matters, it is important to explain the potential tax implications of Class B membership to the Class B members upon issuance of their respective units.

> **2. (a) In the event that at any time (or from time to time) the Managers determine (in their reasonable discretion) that additional funds are required by the Company for or in respect of its business or any of its obligations, expenses, costs, liabilities or expenditures (the "Additional Funds"), then the Managers, acting for and on behalf of, and in the name of, the Company, in the exercise of their**

reasonable discretion and in furtherance of the provisions of Article X-1 hereof, may cause the Company to borrow the Additional funds, with interest payable at then-prevailing rates, from commercial banks, savings and loan associations and/or other lending institutions or from any other Persons, including the Members or Affiliates thereof. In the event that the Company seeks any Additional Funds by way of a loan from a Member, it shall offer such opportunity to all members, *pro rata* in proportion to their respective Percentage Interests (unless Members participating in making any such loan shall agree upon any other ratio).

The effect of subsequent capital contributions of the members, as well as the obligation of members to make subsequent capital contributions is often a significant issue for the members. Generally, members are not required to make additional capital contributions, however, in companies that engage in investment activities, including real estate holding companies, there may be a requirement that each member contribute additional capital (up to a predetermined amount) at the request of the managers.

The provisions of this agreement permit the managers to determine whether additional contributions by the members will be structured as additional capital from the members or as loans. The effect of this is to limit the amount of dilution that will occur if all of the members do not participate, on a *pro rata* basis, in the capital call. This is a "middle of the road" approach that does not result in immediate diminution of the company interest of non-participating members, while still preserving the ability of the members to slowly limit the influence of members who are no longer able to participate actively in the capital needs of the company.

(b) Notwithstanding any provision to the contrary contained in this Agreement, in the event that the Managers are unable or unwilling to cause the Company to borrow the Additional Funds in accordance with the provisions of Article VI-2(a) above, then the Managers, acting for and on behalf of, and in the name of, the Company and in accordance with the provisions of Article X hereof, shall send written notice thereof to each of the Members (a "Call Notice"), which shall set forth the amount of Capital Contributions required, and the Members, *pro rata*, in proportion to their respective Percentage Interests (unless they unanimously agree upon another proportion), shall (and hereby covenant and agree to) contribute such Capital Contributions to the Company within ten (10) business days of the Call Notice (the "Contribution Period"); it being understood and agreed that all such required Additional Funds may be treated as a Capital Contribution and/or loans uniformly, as determined by the Managers, in their sole and absolute discretion.

(c) (i) Notwithstanding any provision contained in this Agreement, in the event that any Member (such Member, hereinafter in this Article VI-2(c), being referred to as the "Defaulting Member") fails to contribute to the Company his proportionate share of the Capital Contributions required under the Call Notice prior to the expiration of the Contribution Period, then each non-Defaulting Member may (but need not) fund such non-Defaulting Member's proportionate share of the defaulted Capital Contribution by way of a Default Loan (as defined below) to or for the benefit of the Defaulting Member.

(ii) If a non-Defaulting Member chooses to fund his proportionate share of the defaulted Capital Contribution by way of a loan, such non-Defaulting Member shall make a Capital Contribution to the Company for the benefit of (and credited to the Capital Account of) the Defaulting Member equal to the principal amount of such loan, which loan shall constitute a recourse advance (a "Default Loan") to the Defaulting Member, the principal of which shall be repayable on or before ninety (90) days from the date of such advance, together with interest thereon at the lesser of (x) an annual rate, compounded quarterly, equal to two (2) times the Prime Rate as of the date of the advance, and (y) the maximum rate permitted by law, and secured, *pro rata* with all other such loans with respect to any such defaulted Capital Contribution, by the Defaulting Member's Company Interest (including any distributions otherwise payable to the Defaulting Member).

(iii) In the event that a Defaulting Member fails to repay all amounts owed with respect to a Default Loan in accordance with Article VI-2(c)(ii) above, time being of the essence, then each non-Defaulting Member that made a Default Loan to the Defaulting Member may elect to purchase a portion of the Defaulting Member's Company Interest by applying all amounts owed by the Defaulting Member with respect to the Default Loan to the purchase price for a portion of the Company Interest theretofore owned by the Defaulting Member. The portion of the Defaulting Member's Company Interest to be purchased as a result of the foregoing shall be equal to the product of (A) the Company Interest of the Defaulting Member, and (B) a fraction, the numerator of which is the dollar amount of the amounts owed by the Defaulting Member to the non-Defaulting Member with respect to the Default Loan, and the denominator of which is the sum of all Capital Contributions of the Defaulting Member plus the Defaulting Member's portion of the Additional Funds that had been called for by the Company through the Call Notice giving rise to such default (whether or not paid in).

(iv) Each Member hereby unconditionally and irrevocably grants to the Company a security interest in such Member's Company Interest to secure such Member's obligation to repay timely any Default Loans deemed made to it pursuant to Article VI-2(c)(ii). The Company shall assign to those non-Defaulting Members making such Default Loans, ratably in proportion to the principal amounts of each such Default Loan, its security interest in a Defaulting Member's Company Interest in order to secure such Default Loans. This Agreement shall be deemed to be a security and pledge agreement in respect of such grant.

(v) To the extent that any portion of a defaulted Capital Contribution is not so funded by non-Defaulting Members, the Defaulting

Member shall remain fully liable to the Company to the extent thereof, plus interest at the lesser of (x) an annual rate, compounded quarterly, equal to two (2) times the Prime Rate as of the date of the advance, and (y) the maximum rate permitted by law, from the date of the default to (but not including) the date of payment.

(vi) Except as otherwise provided herein, no right, power or remedy conferred upon the Company in this Article VI-2(c) shall be exclusive, and each such right, power, or remedy shall be cumulative and in addition to every other right, power or remedy, whether conferred in this Article VI-2(c) or now or hereafter available at law or in equity or by statute or otherwise. No course of dealing between the Company and any Defaulting Member and no delay in exercising any right, power or remedy shall operate as a waiver or otherwise prejudice any such right, power or remedy. The Defaulting Member shall be liable for all expenses and costs (including reasonable attorneys' and other professionals' fees and disbursements) incurred by the Company, the Managers or any non-Defaulting Member in enforcing any of the remedies or rights set forth in this Article VI-2(c). The Company may bring an action against the Defaulting Member to enforce payment of the defaulted Capital Contribution and interest thereon, as well as the payment of all costs and expenses of collection. Each Member acknowledges by its execution of this Agreement that it has been admitted to the Company in reliance upon its agreements that the Company and each other Member may have and exercise any and all rights, powers and remedies provided for in this Article VI-2(c) or otherwise available at law or in equity, and furthermore specifically acknowledges and agrees that, notwithstanding anything to the contrary in this Agreement, the Company shall have the right and power to take such other action as the Managers may deem reasonably necessary or advisable to protect the interests of the Company and the other Members upon a Member's default.

(d) Until such time as the outstanding amount of any Default Loan, together with accrued interest at the aforesaid rate, is repaid in full to the non-Defaulting Member(s), any and all amounts otherwise distributable to the Defaulting Member (or his permitted assigns) under this Agreement (including, without limitation, distributions of Net Cash Flow under Article XII hereof) shall be distributed by the Company to the non-Defaulting Member in satisfaction (in whole or in part) of the Default Loan (the "Designated Distributions").

3. Notwithstanding anything to the contrary contained in this Agreement or under the Act, any issuance of additional Membership Units, other than to employees of the Company in consideration of their services, shall be subject to the following preemptive rights: Each Class A Member shall have the right (but not the obligation) to purchase a portion of any additional Membership Units so issued that is proportionate to such Class A Member's percentage ownership

of Class A Membership Units at the same price, time and terms as for any other Person. If any additional Membership Units are issued, directly or indirectly, to [_____] (each an "Existing Class A Member"), such Existing Class A Member shall be obligated to pay the Fair Market Value for any such Membership Units, without any discount for lack of marketability or minority ownership, unless the Class A Members unanimously agree otherwise.

A pre-emptive right is an important bulwark against dilution for the Class A members. Pre-emptive rights can include various contingencies and be far more complex than the simple pre-emptive rights set forth above; however, the purpose remains the same—to allow the members an opportunity to maintain their respective percentage interest when additional membership units are issued.

4. Each Member that is a holder of Membership Units in the Company shall be entitled to have a certificate, signed by the Managers of the Company, exhibiting the number of Membership Units in the Company owned by such Member. All certificates representing Membership Units which are subject to restrictions on transfer or to other restrictions may have imprinted thereon such notation to such effect as may be determined by the Managers.

Given the differences between "shares" in a corporation and "membership units" in an LLC, membership units are not always certificated like corporate shares. Whether an LLC will require or permit certification of membership units is a matter to be agreed upon by the members. Importantly, if members intend to pledge their respective interest in the LLC as security for other obligation, certificated membership units will be necessary so that the certificates can be delivered to a secured party that is seeking to perfect its security interest in the pledged membership units.

5. **No Member shall be required to make any Capital Contribution to the Company beyond the amounts set forth in this Article VI, except as may be agreed to by such Member in writing.**

Typically, the members of an LLC are not required to make capital contributions other than their initial capital contribution. However, an operating agreement can require capital contributions by the members in predetermined amounts, or in amounts to be determined by the managers pursuant to a capital call. If participation in capital calls is mandatory, the operating agreement must also address the consequences of not participating (i.e., dilution, default, dismissal).

6. **Except as provided in this Agreement, no interest shall accrue or be payable to any Member by reason of such Member's Capital Contribution or such Member's Capital Account.**

The capital account of a member generally does not accrue interest, however, the operating agreement can provide for a preferred return to a member or class of members if there are economic reasons to do so (as we have in this case).

7. **Notwithstanding any inferences to the contrary in this Agreement, no Member (in such Member's capacity as a member) shall be personally liable for losses, costs, expenses, liabilities or obligations of the Company, nor shall any Manager be personally liable for losses, costs, expenses, liabilities or obligations of the Company.**

One of the purposes of establishing a limited liability company is to limit the personal liability of the members with respect to the business activities and obligations of the limited liability company. Under Delaware law, a member is not personally liable for the obligations of the company; however, a member maintains personal liability for any capital contribution requirements in the operating agreement, any "bad acts" of the member, and for any personal guaranties offered by the member for the benefit of the company.

8.   The foregoing provisions of this Article VI are not
     intended to be for the benefit of any creditor or
     other person or entity (other than a Member in his
     or her capacity as a member of the Company) to
     whom   or   which   any   debts,   liabilities   or
     obligations are owed by (or who or which
     otherwise has any claim against) the Company or
     any of the Members; and no such creditor or other
     person or entity shall obtain any right under any
     of the foregoing provisions against the Company
     or any of the Managers or Members by reason of
     any debt, liability or obligation (or otherwise).

The intent of the language of Section 8 is to reinforce the limited personal
liability of members with respect to the obligations of the limited liability
company and confirm that creditors of the company may not use the
capital obligations and concepts of Article VI to recover from the
members individually.

ARTICLE VII

Allocation of Profit and Loss

1.   "Profit" and "Loss" shall, for purposes of this
     Agreement, mean, for each fiscal year of the
     Company or other period, an amount equal to the
     Company's taxable income, gain, loss or
     deduction for such year or period, determined by
     the Company's certified public accountants in
     accordance with I.R.C. Section 703(a), with the
     following adjustments:

     (a) All income or gain of the Company that is
         exempt from Federal income tax and not
         otherwise taken into account in computing
         Profit and Loss pursuant to this Article VII-1
         shall be added to such taxable income, gain,
         loss or deduction.

(b) Any expenditure of the Company described in I.R.C. Section 705(a)(2)(B) or treated as an expenditure described in such Section and not otherwise taken into account in computing Profit and Loss pursuant to this Article VII shall be subtracted from such taxable income, gain, loss or deduction.

2. Subject to the provisions of Article VII-3 hereof, the distributive shares of each item of Profit and Loss (or, if necessary, items thereof) for any Company Accounting Year or other period shall be allocated to each Member *pro rata*, in accordance with each Member's Percentage Interest.

Profits and losses can be allocated in a number of ways. The *pro rata* allocation proposed here is a simple and straightforward method whereby the members are each allocated their *pro rata* portion of profits or losses at the end of each year. Under this method, a member's capital account balance is increased based on their *pro rata* portion of profits, and decreased based upon their *pro rata* portion of losses.

3. The Company, with the review and concurrence of the Company's certified public accountants, shall allocate taxable income, gain, loss, credit, deduction (or items thereof) arising in any Company Accounting Year in a manner other than as provided in Article VII-2 hereof if, and to the extent that, the allocations otherwise provided under this Article VII would not be permissible under I.R.C. Sections 704(b) and/or 704(c). Any allocation made pursuant to and in accordance with this Article VII-3 shall be deemed to be a complete substitute for the allocation otherwise provided in Article VII-2 hereof, and no amendment of this Agreement shall be required with respect thereto, and each Member shall, for all purposes and in all respects, be deemed to

> have approved any such reasonable allocation,
> unless such allocation under this Article VII-3
> would, or could, have a materially adverse effect
> on the balance of each Member's Capital Account
> relative to the balance of each Member's Capital
> Account had the allocation been made as
> provided for under Article VII-2 hereof.

Allocations of profit and loss to the members must be consistent with the Internal Revenue Code. The current language of Section 704(b) requires that allocations to partners have "substantial economic effect." Section 704(c) sets forth the allocation method for property that is contributed to the company at a value that is different from the basis for such property. Article VII (3) allows the members, in consultation with the company's accountants, to revise the allocation methods of the company if I.R.C. Sections 704(b) or 704(c) are changed so that the company is able to comply with such changes without amending the operating agreement.

> 4. If a Company Interest is transferred or assigned
> during a Company Accounting Year, that part of
> any item of Profit, Loss, income, gain, deduction,
> credit or basis allocated pursuant to this Article
> VII with respect to the Company Interest so
> transferred shall, in the reasonable discretion of
> the Managers, either (i) be based on
> segmentization of the Company Accounting Year
> between the transferor and the transferee or (ii) be
> allocated between the transferor and the
> transferee in proportion to the number of days in
> such Company Accounting Year during which
> each owned such Company Interest, as disclosed
> by the Company's books and records.

The IRC provides different methods for allocating profit and loss when a company interest is transferred mid-year. The predominant methods are to either (1) close the books as of the day of the transfer and allocate profit and loss based on the actual performance of the company as of that day, or (2) aggregate the performance of the company for the entire year, and then allocate a *pro rata* portion of such performance to the transferor and the transferee based on the respective portion of the year that each held the company interest.

ARTICLE VIII

Withdrawal of Member

1. In furtherance of the provisions of the Act, and except as otherwise set forth herein, no Member shall have the right, power or authority to withdraw from the Company or to demand and receive property of the Company or any distribution in return for such Member's Capital Contribution or Capital Account, prior to the dissolution and winding up of the Company.

2. Except as otherwise may be permitted under Articles XIII, XIV and XVI hereof, in the event that any Member withdraws from the Company in breach of this Agreement (including specifically, the provisions of Article VIII-1 above), such withdrawal shall, *ipso facto*, without any further action by the Company, the Managers or any other Members, constitute a default by the withdrawing Member under this Agreement, for which the Company and the other Members shall have all of their rights and remedies, at law or in equity, under this Agreement or under applicable law, including, without limitation, the right to recover damages, including, without limitation, reasonable attorneys' and paralegals' fees, from such withdrawing Member, which damages may offset the amount otherwise distributable to such withdrawing Member under the terms of this Agreement (including, without limitation, the provisions of Article XII hereof).

The right of a member to withdraw from an LLC is governed by the operating agreement, and Delaware courts have demonstrated a willingness to uphold restrictions and/or prohibitions on the withdrawal of a member. If withdrawal is prohibited, as it is in this agreement, a member who attempts to withdraw may be found to be in breach of the operating agreement, and the default provisions of the operating agreement may be invoked, resulting in suspension or diminution of distributions, or even divestiture of the withdrawing member's membership interest.

ARTICLE IX

Legal Title to Company Assets

1. **Legal title to the Company Assets shall be held in the name of the Company or in any other manner which the Managers reasonably determine to be in the best interests of the Company.**

One of the benefits of a limited liability company is the lack of required formalities, as compared to a traditional corporation. This informality, however, can lead to members ignoring the entity form and merging personal and company assets, or using company assets improperly as personal assets. As with corporations, limited liability company members risk a piercing of the "corporate veil" if the form of the company is not properly maintained. To avoid this risk, clear lines of demarcation must exist between personal and company assets. This means, at a minimum, the requirement of a separate company bank account, titling company assets in the name of the company, borrowing in the name of the company (often with the personal guaranties of the members), executing documents in the name of the company and enforcing proper authorization of material expenditures.

2. **It is expressly understood and agreed that the manner of holding title to the Company Assets is solely for the convenience of the Company. Accordingly, the spouse, heirs, executors or administrators, distributees, directors, officers, stockholders, members, managers, successors or assigns of any Member shall have no right, title or**

interest in or to any of the Company Assets by
reason of the manner in which title is held; rather,
the Company Assets shall be subject to the terms
of this Agreement. It is further understood and
agreed that the Members' Company Interest shall
be considered personalty and not a real property
interest; accordingly, the Members shall not have
the right to demand or request a partition (or
similar division) of any of the Company Assets.

ARTICLE X

Management; Indemnification

A limited liability company can be managed by the members or by a
manager(s) appointed by the members. If all members intend to participate
actively and equally in the management of the company, then member-
management is appropriate and equitable. If, however, it is expected that
one member will manage the company, or if all the members intend to take
a more passive role in the management of the company, then it is
appropriate to have the company be manager-managed, instead of member-
managed. We advise our clients to utilize manager-managed LLCs because
this construct provides the most flexibility. When members are involved in
the management of the company, it is important to draw distinctions clearly
between actions that are "member actions" and those that are "manager
actions." This can be challenging when the members wear more than one
hat with respect to the operation of the company. As a general rule, the
company records should have separate minutes and resolutions of member
and manager meetings or, at the very least, important company actions
should be styled as "joint action of the members and the manager(s)" so
that it is clear which level of company governance authority has been
invoked with respect to a particular action. This can be particularly
meaningful with respect to statutory requirements with respect to approval
of the members and/or manager(s).

1.   (a) Except as otherwise expressly provided in this
           Agreement, all management powers and decisions
           of the Company shall be exercised by or under the

authority of, and the business and affairs of the Company shall be managed under the direction of, the Managers, who shall have all rights, powers and authority permitted by the laws of the State of Delaware as "managers" (as such term is defined and applied under the Act), and all decisions made for and on behalf of the Company by the Members shall be binding upon the Company. The Managers (acting for and on behalf of the Company), in extension and not in limitation of the rights and powers given them by law or by the other provisions of this Agreement, shall, in their reasonable discretion, have the full and entire right, power and authority, in the management of the Company business, to do any and all acts and things necessary, proper, convenient or advisable to effectuate the purposes of the Company, including, without limitation, negotiating the terms and conditions of contracts between the Company and the third party vendors, electing new Members, and establishing performance-based equity incentives for employees of the Company. The Managers shall devote [*his full time and attention*] to the management of the business of the Company [*such efforts and professional attention as reasonably necessary for the efficient operation of the Company business*]. Any and all actions and/or decisions made for or on behalf of the Company by the Managers in accordance with the terms of this Agreement shall be made by a majority-in-number of the Managers and shall be binding upon the Company and the Members. In furtherance of the foregoing, any one of the Managers may execute documents and take other actions on behalf of the Company, which shall bind the Company when authorized by action of the Company pursuant to the provisions of this Agreement.

As demonstrated by the italicized optional language above, the expected scope of the manager's attention to the company can vary, depending on the agreements among the members. For entrepreneurs involved in a start-up company, "full time and attention" may mean seventy hours a week, whereas the manager of a more established company, or side business, may only be expected to do what is "reasonably necessary for the efficient operation" of the company, which may mean fifteen to twenty hours a week. Ultimately, it is a fact and circumstance specific determination.

> **(b) In the event that there is an even number of Managers, any and all actions and/or decisions of such Managers with respect to the management and/or control of the Company and the Company business shall be taken or made jointly by such Managers, which actions and/or decisions shall be binding upon the Members and the Company. Notwithstanding the foregoing or anything to the contrary contained herein (including, without limitation, the provisions of Article XVIII-3 hereof), in the event of a dispute, disagreement or deadlock between the Managers with respect to any material decision and/or action in connection with the management of the Company and the Company business, which the Managers are not able to resolve themselves after using their best efforts to do so (the "Disputed Issue"), then the Managers shall submit the Disputed Issue to binding arbitration, in which event the resolution of the Disputed Issue shall be made in accordance with the rules, regulations and procedures of the American Arbitration Association (as applicable in the State of Delaware). The resolution of any Disputed Issue by arbitration hereunder shall be final, binding and conclusive upon the Company, the Managers and the Members.**

An even number of managers can result in deadlock for the company if there is not a clear method for resolving deadlocked decisions. The provisions of this agreement contemplate submission of a deadlocked issue to an arbiter, however, there are a number of methods that can be adopted to address deadlocks—a designated third party can be appointed to decide the decision, the decision can be submitted to the members, one of the managers can be given the "casting vote" in deadlock situations, or a majority member can be designated as the deciding party.

Additional Provision

(c) *Notwithstanding anything to the contrary contained in this Agreement, the following is an exclusive list of major decisions that require the vote of a majority-in-Class A Units of the Class A Members entitled to vote. The Class A Members' authority and responsibility in voting on the following matters may not be delegated to any one or a group of Class A Members or officers or any committee established by the Managers:*

(i) *a sale of the Company (by way of merger, equity sale or asset sale, as the case may be);*

(ii) *the hiring and compensation of any management-level employee at a rate of compensation that exceeds the annual compensation of the Company's Chief Executive Officer;*

(iii) *effectuating an initial public offering of the Company's securities;*

(iv) *liquidating, winding up or dissolving the Company; and*

(v) *commencing a formal bankruptcy proceeding involving the Company.*

This is a very short list of so-called "major decision" rights. We have drafted this list to be as short as five matters and, depending on the complexity of the governance structure or the company's business, as long as thirty such matters.

> 2. (a) Any Manager designated hereunder may resign at any time by giving written notice to the other Managers and the Members at least thirty (30) days prior to the effective date of such resignation; provided, however, that, notwithstanding the foregoing or anything to the contrary contained in this Agreement or under the Act, in no event shall any Manager designated hereunder be removed by the Members, unless such Manager engages in fraud or willful misconduct and the Members (other than a Member who is also the Manager that engaged in such fraud or willful misconduct) unanimously agree and consent to such removal.

Removal provisions too can vary widely depending on the dynamic between the company's members. We provide above a limited removal right in the event that the manager commits "bad acts."

> (b) In the event of the death, adjudication of insanity or incompetency, resignation or retirement of any Manager designated hereunder, the Members owning at least fifty-one percent (51%) of the total number of issued and outstanding Membership Units may appoint one (1) or more successor Managers, who shall have the right, power and authority to manage, oversee and administer the business and affairs of the Company in accordance with the provisions of this Agreement. No Person designated to serve as a Manager hereunder is required to be either a

> Member of the Company or a resident (or domestic corporation) of the State of Delaware.

The events that lead to the removal of a manager are based on the individual facts and circumstances selected by the members when preparing the operating agreement, and the enforcement and interpretation of such provisions will inevitably be a matter of interpretation for the managers and members when such events occur. Given the potential conflicts that may arise on the withdrawal of a manager, the events giving rise to such withdrawal should be defined as clearly as possible beforehand, so that the potential for conflicting personal interpretations is limited as much as possible.

> 3. Notwithstanding anything to the contrary contained in this Agreement, the following is an exclusive list of major decisions that require the vote of a majority-in-Class A Units of the Class A Members entitled to vote. The Class A Members' authority and responsibility in voting on the following matters may not be delegated to any one or a group of Class A Members or officers or any committee established by the Managers:
>
> (a) a sale of the Company (by way of merger, equity sale or asset sale, as the case may be);
>
> (b) the hiring and compensation of any management-level employee at a rate of compensation that exceeds the annual compensation of the Company's Chief Executive Officer;
>
> (c) effectuating an initial public offering of the Company's securities;
>
> (d) liquidating, winding up or dissolving the Company; and
>
> (e) commencing a formal bankruptcy proceeding involving the Company.

4. (a) In furtherance of (but not in limitation of) the
provisions of this Article X, the Members have
the right, power and authority to designate one
(1) or more persons (whether or not a Member)
to serve as executive Officers of the Company,
including, without limitation, the designation
of persons to serve as Chief Executive Officer,
President, Vice President or Vice Presidents,
Secretary, Treasurer and such other officers as
the Members shall deem necessary or
appropriate, who shall exercise such powers
and perform such duties as shall from time to
time be defined and determined by the
Members, in their sole and absolute discretion.
Any number of offices may be held by the same
person. The Chief Executive Officer shall be
responsible for supervision and direction of the
day-to-day operations of the Company and
shall report directly to, and be subject to the
review and authority of, the Managers.

(b) Any Officer initially appointed hereunder or
otherwise elected or appointed by the
Members may be terminated and removed,
with or without cause, at any time by the
Members. Any vacancy occurring in any office
of the Company may (but shall not be
required to) be filled by the Members.

Many clients insist on language regarding officer positions because it is what
they are used to seeing in corporations and officer positions are more often
used for business card and marketing purposes.

5. Unless otherwise provided herein, neither the
Members nor any Officer shall be entitled to
receive any payments, fees or other compensation
for serving as a Member or Officer hereunder.

6. (a) [_____] is hereby designated the "Tax Matters Partner" (as such term is defined and used under the I.R.C. and the Treasury Regulations thereunder) of the Company.

   (b) The Tax Matters Partner of the Company shall, within fifteen (15) business days of receipt thereof, forward to each Member a photocopy of any correspondence relating to the Company received from the Internal Revenue Service which relates to matters that are of material importance to the Company and/or its Members. The Tax Matters Partner of the Company shall, within fifteen (15) business days thereof, advise each Member in writing of the substance of any conversation held with any representative of the Internal Revenue Service which relates to matters that are of material importance to the Company and/or its Members.

   (c) Any reasonable costs incurred by the Tax Matters Partner of the Company for retaining accountants, lawyers and/or other professionals on behalf of the Company in connection with dealing with the Internal Revenue Service on behalf of or with respect to the Company shall, upon the review of the Company's independent certified public accountants, be expenses of the Company; provided, however, that the Tax Matters Partner shall not incur any professional fees or expenses on behalf of the Company without the prior written approval of the Members.

The designation of one of the members as "tax matters partner" imparts to that member the authority to interact with the Internal Revenue Service on behalf of the company with respect to tax issues. Given the pass-through nature of LLCs, the company is likely to have limited IRS interactions, primarily dealing with the any payroll/employee-related tax issues, and the Schedule K-1s delivered to the members.

7. In furtherance of the provisions of this Article X, the Managers may cause the Company to contract with any Person, including, without limitation, any of the Members, any entity in which any of the Members may have an interest and/or any Affiliated entity, at reasonable and competitive rates of compensation, commission or remuneration, for the performance of any and all services which may at any time be necessary, proper, convenient or advisable to carry on the business of the Company.

8. The Managers shall be fully and entirely reimbursed by the Company for any and all reasonable out-of-pocket costs and expenses incurred by the Managers in connection with the formation of the Company, the acquisition and transfer of the Company Assets and/or the management and supervision of the Company business; provided, however, that, with respect to any such reimbursement, the Managers shall present the Company with such invoices, in such detail and with such receipts, as are necessary to substantiate such out-of-pocket costs and expenses.

9. (a) The Managers and any authorized Officer (each an "Indemnified Party") shall be indemnified and held harmless by the Company from and against any and all claims, demands, liabilities, costs, expenses, damages and causes of action, of any nature whatsoever, arising out of or incidental to the management and supervision of the Company affairs, the acquisition of any Company Assets

or as otherwise permitted under the Act, except where the claim at issue is based upon the gross negligence, fraud or willful misconduct of the Indemnified Party.

(b) No Indemnified Party shall be liable, responsible or accountable in damages or otherwise to the Members or to the Company for any acts performed by such Indemnified Party in good faith and within the scope of this Agreement; provided, however, that, as noted in Article X-8(a) above, an Indemnified Party shall be liable for his actions and/or omissions to the extent the same are attributable to the gross negligence, fraud or willful misconduct of such Indemnified Party. No Indemnified Party shall be contractually liable under this Agreement or under the Act for the return of the Capital Account of any Member.

(c) The indemnification authorized by this Article X-8 shall include, but not be limited to, payment of (i) reasonable attorneys' and paralegals' fees or other expenses incurred in connection with settlement or in any finally adjudicated legal proceeding and (ii) the removal of any liens affecting any property of the indemnitee.

(d) The indemnification rights contained in this Article X-8 shall be cumulative of, and in addition to, any and all rights, remedies and recourses to which an Indemnified Party shall be entitled, whether pursuant to the provisions of this Agreement, at law or in equity. Indemnifications shall be made solely and entirely from the Company Assets, and no Member shall be personally liable to any

> indemnitee under this Article X-8. Furthermore, the provisions of this Article X-8 are not intended to be for the benefit of any creditor or other Person to whom or which any debts, liabilities or obligations are owed by (or who or which otherwise has a claim against) the indemnitee, and no such creditor or other Person shall obtain any right under the provisions of this Article X-8 against the Company or any Member by reason of any debt, liability or obligation of (or other claim against) the indemnitee.

The indemnification standard in a limited liability company agreement should align with the fiduciary obligations required among managers, members, and the company. For example, if a manager is indemnified in all cases *except* willful misconduct or gross negligence, then the indemnification provisions create a higher (or lower, depending on your viewpoint) standard for managers as between a manager, the company, and the members than the simple negligence duty of care standard that we believe is customary.

ARTICLE XI

Bank Accounts; Books and Records; Tax Elections

As noted above, the company must maintain a separate existence from the members to preserve the personal liability shield for the members. In short, this means that separate ledger, books, payable and bank accounts must be maintained for the company, and the funds and obligations of the members and the company should never be comingled. If there is more than one member, no single member should be able to exercise a disproportionate amount of control over the bank accounts or invested funds of the company, including the withdrawal of company funds for personal uses.

> 1. The funds of the Company shall be deposited in such separate bank or investment account or accounts as shall be determined by the Managers, in their sole discretion, and the Managers shall

arrange for the appropriate conduct of such account or accounts.

2. The books and records of the Company shall be kept, and the financial condition and the results of its operations recorded, in accordance with the accounting methods elected to be followed by the Company for Federal income tax purposes. The books and records of the Company shall reflect all Company transactions and shall be appropriate and adequate for the Company's business. The fiscal year of the Company for financial reporting and for Federal income tax purposes shall be the Company Accounting Year.

Limited liability companies can elect to be treated as a corporation or a partnership for tax purposes. In almost all cases, the members elect to have the company treated as a partnership, which results in pass-through taxation in which no tax liabilities are incurred by the company, and all losses and gains of the company are "passed through" to the members, who each recognize their *pro rata* portion of profits and losses as individual income on their annual personal tax returns. Given this status, the tax recordkeeping obligations of the company typically involve the proper accounting of annual results of operations and the allocation of such financial results among the members on their respective Schedule K-1s.

3. The Company shall keep at its principal office or at such other or additional offices (either within or without the State of Delaware) as the Managers shall deem advisable (a) books and records setting forth a current list of the full name and last known address of each Member, (b) a copy of the Certificate and this Agreement, and all amendments thereto, (c) copies of the Company's Federal, state and local income tax returns and personal property or intangible property tax returns, if any, for the three (3) most recent Company Accounting Years, (d) copies of any

**financial statements of the Company for the three
(3) most recent Company Accounting Years,
which reflect the Company's state of business and
financial condition during such periods and (e)
any other information and/or records required by
the Act. Each Member (and such Member's duly
authorized representative) shall have access to the
books and records of the Company and the right
to inspect and copy them, provided such request
is reasonable and made at least five (5) business
days in advance of such inspection, is done at
reasonable hours and is done at such Member's
personal expense.**

Under Section 18-305[1] of the Delaware Limited Liability Company Act,[2] a
Member of an LLC has a statutory right to review:

(1) True and full information regarding the status of the business and
financial condition of the limited liability company;

(2) Promptly after becoming available, a copy of the limited liability
company's federal, state and local income tax returns for each year;

(3) A current list of the name and last known business, residence, or
mailing address of each member and manager;

(4) A copy of any written limited liability company agreement and
certificate of formation and all amendments thereto, together with
executed copies of any written powers of attorney pursuant to
which the limited liability company agreement and any certificate
and all amendments thereto have been executed;

(5) True and full information regarding the amount of cash and a
description and statement of the agreed value of any other property
or services contributed by each member and which each member

---

[1] DEL. CODE ANN. tit. 6, §18-305 (West 2010).
[2] Delaware Limited Liability Company Act, DEL. CODE. ANN. tit. 6, ch. 18 (West 2010).

has agreed to contribute in the future, and the date on which each became a member; and

(6) Other information regarding the affairs of the limited liability company as is just and reasonable.

While an operating agreement cannot be any more restrictive than the statute, Delaware courts have upheld operating agreement provisions limiting the member's access to the books and records of the company to those enumerated items. Those provisions that take a broader view of the records that members may inspect, such as the provision above, have been held to include a right to inspect the general ledger and any other relevant records of the company.

> **4. If there is a distribution of the Company Assets (or any portion thereof) as described in I.R.C. Section 734, or if there is a transfer of any Company Interests as described in I.R.C. Section 743, then, upon the request of any Member, the Managers may (but shall not be required to) cause the Company to file an election under I.R.C. Section 754 to provide for an optional adjustment to the basis of Company Assets. Moreover, notwithstanding the possible future applicability of the provisions of I.R.C. Section 761(a), it is understood that no election shall be made by the Company or any Member to be excluded from the application of the provisions of Subtitle A, Chapter 1, Subchapter K of the I.R.C.**

Elections under Section 754 of the Internal Revenue Code are a complex area of tax law and an in-depth discussion of such elections is beyond the scope of this book. In essence, a 754 election is made to equalize the inside and outside basis of a member of an LLC. Without a 754 election, certain members (particularly a member who purchased their units from an existing or prior member) can experience disproportionate gains, as well as disproportionate limits on depreciation deductions. Making a 754 election can have a material effect on the value of LLC assets, and can result in a

significant recordkeeping burden, therefore, experienced tax counsel should
be consulted before such an election is made.

ARTICLE XII

Distributions

1. **Notwithstanding anything to the contrary, the
    Managers (on behalf of the Company) shall, unless
    there are insufficient funds available, distribute to
    each Member at the conclusion of each Company
    Accounting Year (or within ninety (90) days
    thereafter), an amount equal to such Member's Tax
    Liability (provided that the Managers shall be under
    no obligation to cause the Company to borrow, lend
    or contribute to the Company the funds necessary to
    make such distributions).**

As discussed above, members of limited liability companies that elect to be
treated as a partnership for tax purposes must include their *pro rata* portion of
the profits of the company on their individual tax returns. Therefore, such
members run the risk of recognizing income without receiving actual cash with
which to pay the accompanying tax liabilities, (i.e., so-called "phantom"
income). The tax distribution addressed in XII-1 above is intended to avoid
phantom income by mandating distributions to the members in an amount
equal to the estimated combined federal and state tax liabilities of the members.
This provision can be adjusted to provide that such distributions are mandatory
only in years in which the company records a profit, thereby further restricting
the possibility for members to receive any mandatory "windfall" distributions
without accompanying tax liabilities.

2. **Except to the extent Net Cash Flow shall be
    distributed upon termination of the Company
    pursuant to Article XV-2 hereof, all Net Cash
    Flow generated during a Company Accounting
    Year shall be distributed at such time or times as
    the Members may determine, in their reasonable
    discretion, during such Company Accounting
    Year in the following order of priority:**

(a) First, to the Class A Members, an amount equal to any respective accrued and unpaid Preferred Return;

(b) Second to the Class A Members, aggregate amounts equal to any respective Additional Capital Contributions (if any);

(c) Third, to the Class A Members, aggregate amounts equal to any respective Net Capital Investment; and

(d) Finally, any and all remaining Net Cash Flow shall be distributed to the Members, *pro rata*, in proportion to their respective number of Membership Units in relation to the total number of issued and outstanding Membership Units.

The cash flow waterfall can be structured in any way the members agree to reflect accurately the priorities and/or preferred returns to which the members are entitled. Typically, as demonstrated above, the waterfall will reflect a priority of distribution to the members who have made capital contributions to the company, as compared to the members who have not contributed capital in exchange for their units (in this case, the Class B members).

3. All distributions made within the Company Accounting Year shall be subject to adjustment by reference to the financial statements for such Company Accounting Year. If any additional amount is to be distributed by reason of such financial statements, such additional amount shall be deemed a distribution for such Company Accounting Year; and if any excess amount was distributed during such Company Accounting Year, as reflected by such financial statements, the excess amount shall be taken into account in reducing subsequent distributions.

The language in XII-3 is intended to serve as savings language that will allow the company to adjust future distributions to reflect any overpayments made by the company in prior distributions. Note that this language allows "recovery" of amounts that were previously distributed to a member if such distributions were in excess of such member's *pro rata* portion of profits, as stated in the company's year-end financial statements. The language is not connected to the mandatory tax distribution amounts, and does permit recovery of distributions that were made in excess of a member's tax liability if the distributions did not exceed the member's pro-rata portion of profits.

ARTICLE XIII

Assignability of Company Interests

1. (a) Subject to the provisions of Articles XIII-2, XIV and XVI hereof, no Member shall sell, assign, transfer, convey, pledge, encumber, or in any way alienate or dispose of all or any portion of such Member's Company Interest, without delivering to the other Members a notice setting forth the terms and conditions of the proposed transfer and obtaining the prior written consent of the Managers (which consent shall be sole and absolute); provided, however, that such prior written consent shall not be required with respect to any transfers by a Member of all or any part of his, her or its Company Interest to any Permitted Transferee. Notwithstanding anything to the contrary contained in this Agreement, an assignee of a Member (including, without limitation, any Permitted Transferee) shall not become a Substituted Member unless: (x) the assigning Member so provides in the instrument of assignment, (y) the assignee agrees in writing to be bound by the provisions of this Agreement, and (z) the assigning Member, the Managers, the assignee

and any other required signatory parties execute an amendment to this Agreement, which shall reflect, among other things, the admission of the assignee as a Substituted Member and the withdrawal of the assigning Member from the Company. Notwithstanding the foregoing, no such transfer to a Permitted Transferee or any other sale, transfer, conveyance, pledge or encumbrance will be permitted if such event would result in a violation of any applicable securities laws, as determined by the Managers.

The provisions of this operating agreement limit the ability of a member to transfer their company interest, but do not prohibit all transfers of company interests. Members are permitted to transfer the economic interests related to such member's company interests to the specifically enumerated "permitted transferees." These transfers, however, do not transfer the voting or management control relating to the company interests, and the transferring member retains those rights. Moreover, while the agreement contains a right of first refusal among the members, there is no blanket prohibition on transfers of company interests. This structure is in keeping with decisions by the Delaware courts that have reinforced the principle that operating agreements cannot contain a comprehensive restraint on alienation of company interests. Any provisions that seek to do so will likely not be enforceable in Delaware.

(b) Notwithstanding the provisions of Article XIII-1(a) hereof, but subject to the provisions of Article XIII-2 hereof, in the event that a Member desires to sell, assign, transfer, convey, pledge, encumber, or in any way alienate all or any portion of his, her or its Company Interest, such Member must first give to the other Members (the "Offeree Members") notice of his, her or its intention to make such disposition, which notice shall specify the purchase price and payment terms (including collateral to secure the payment of

> any deferred payments) upon which the Offeror Member is willing to sell his, her or its Company Interest (the "Offer").

Paragraph 1(b) of Article XIII sets forth the terms of the right of first refusal given to the members. The first step in the right of first refusal assumes that the member seeking to transfer the company interest has received a bona fide offer to purchase such member's company interest and, thereafter, provides notice to the other members of the terms of the bona fide offer.

> For a period of thirty (30) days from the receipt of such notice (the "Election Period"), the Offeree Members, *pro rata*, in proportion to the respective number of Membership Units owned by the Offeree Members in relation to the total number of issued and outstanding Membership Units (unless they agree upon another proportion), shall have the option (but not the obligation) to elect to purchase the Offering Member's Company Interest (or portion thereof) at the same price and upon the same terms and conditions as are set forth in the Offer. The Offer shall be in effect and irrevocable for the entire Election Period, during which the Offeror Member shall be prohibited from selling or otherwise disposing of his, her or its Company Interest (or portion thereof). If the Offeree Members (or any of them) choose(s) to accept the Offer, such Offeree Member(s) shall so notify the Offeror Member within the Election Period and closing shall take place at a mutually agreed time, place and date not later than ninety (90) days after such election.

Once the member seeking to transfer the company interest provides notice to the other members, the other members have thirty days to exercise their rights to purchase the offered company interest, at the same price and terms as contained in the bona fide offer. If all the remaining members elect to exercise their respective right to purchase the offered company interest, then each member is permitted to purchase a *pro rata* portion of the company interest in an amount equal to their respective ownership percentages (calculated without inclusion of the offered company interest). If not all the members elect to exercise their right to purchase the company interest, then those members electing to purchase the company interest may agree on the respective portion of the offered company interest to be purchased by each such member.

> **If such notice has not been given by the Offeree Member(s) prior to the expiration of the Election Period, or if the Offeree Member(s) do(es) not agree to purchase the Offeror Member's Company Interest (or portion thereof), the Offeror Member shall be free to dispose of his, her or its Company Interest to a third party, who or which is not Affiliated with the Offeror Member and is financially capable of carrying out the terms and conditions of the sale; provided, however, that any such disposition shall be made within one hundred twenty (120) days after the expiration of the Election Period; and provided, further, that such disposition shall be made for a purchase price no less than that contained in the Offer and on other terms and conditions at least as favorable to the Offeror Member as those contained in the Offer.**

If, after the thirty-day period, the members have not purchased all of the offered company interest, then the member may sell the company interest (or any remaining portion) to the third party on the terms set forth in the notice.

> **In the event that the Offeror Member's Company Interest is not so disposed of within said one hundred twenty (120)-day period, the**

> provisions of this Article XIII-1(b) shall again
> be applicable and must be complied with.

If the offered company interest is not sold within 120 days of the end of the thirty-day right of first refusal period, or if the terms of the bona fide offer materially change prior to consummation of the sale, then the right of first refusal process described in 1(b) must be complied with again before the sale to the third party can be completed.

> 2. Notwithstanding anything contained in this Agreement to the contrary, it is expressly understood and agreed that no transfer of any Company Interests shall be made if such transfer would, or could, (i) jeopardize the partnership tax status of the Company for Federal and state income tax purposes or otherwise cause the Company to be treated as a publicly-traded partnership for Federal income tax purposes, (ii) result in a termination of the Company within the meaning of I.R.C. Section 708(b) unless all Members consent in writing to such transfer or substitution, or (iii) violate or cause the Company to violate, any state or Federal securities law or any other applicable law or governmental rule or regulation.

A limited number of events could jeopardize the tax status of a limited liability company. If the company's membership were to grow so large that it became a "publicly traded partnership," then its tax status would be affected. Similarly, under I.R.C. Section 708(b),[3] a transfer of more than 50 percent of the company interests in the company is a "technical termination" for tax purposes, which results in the termination of the tax year for the "old" limited liability company on the day of the transfer, and starts a new tax year for the "new" limited liability company on the day after. While not a significant issue, it does create some administrative burdens for the members, therefore the requirement that tax terminations be approved by the members.

---

[3] I.R.C. § 708(b) (2012).

3. Notwithstanding anything to the contrary contained in this Agreement, the Managers shall not have the right to admit additional Members to the Company without the prior unanimous consent of the Members. Any authorized admission of additional Members under this Article XIII-4 (in contrast to an assignment of an existing Company Interest under Article XIII-1 hereof) shall dilute, *pro rata*, all Company Interests of the Members existing at the time of such admission.

The managers are properly vested with the authority to manage the business of the company; however, the managers are not given the authority to make decisions that affect the economic interest of the members. The introduction of new members, and the accompanying dilution, has a significant impact on the respective economic interest of the members and, as such, is a decision that is reserved to the members' (in this case unanimous) discretion.

4. Unless named in this Agreement or otherwise admitted to the Company in accordance with the terms of this Agreement, no Person shall be considered a Member. The Company, the Managers, each Member and any other Persons having business with the Company need deal only with Members so named or so admitted; they shall not be required to deal with any other Person by reason of an assignment by a Member or by reason of the termination of a Member, except as otherwise provided in this Agreement. In the absence of the substitution of a Member for an assigning or terminated Member, any payment to a Member or to his, her or its legal representatives shall acquit the Company, the Managers and the Members of all liability to any other Person(s) who or which may be interested in such payment by reason of an assignment by, or the termination of, such Member.

The provisions of Article XIII-4 clarify that an assignment of economic interest to a permitted transferee under 1(a) above, or a transfer in violation of the operating agreement, does not vest the transferee with the authority to act in the name of the company, or to engage third parties on behalf of the company. Only those members who are properly admitted to the company may act as a member of the company. This language protects the members, managers, and officers of the company from being required to treat a non-member as a member under the operating agreement.

ARTICLE XIV

Bankruptcy of a Member

In the event of the Bankruptcy of a Member (the "Bankrupt Member"), the other Members (the "Continuing Members"), in accordance with their respective number of Membership Units in relation to the total number of issued and outstanding Membership Units (unless they agree upon another proportion), shall have the option (but not the obligation), exercisable by giving notice thereof to the Bankrupt Member or to such Bankrupt Member's trustee in Bankruptcy, guardian, receiver or other legal representative, to purchase all (but not less than all) of the Bankrupt Member's Company Interest, within ninety (90) days after the event of such Bankruptcy, at a price equal to the Fair Market Value of such Company Interest as determined in accordance with Article I hereof. Within sixty (60) days after the joint written report required to determine the Fair Market Value of such Bankrupt Member's Company Interest or written report of the third (3rd) appraiser (as the case may be) has been rendered, the Continuing Members shall give notice to the legal representative of the Bankrupt Member of their decision as to the exercise of the aforesaid option. If such option is exercised, settlement shall be held within thirty (30) days from the date of such exercise. The terms of payment shall be all cash or as otherwise agreed upon by the respective parties.

To avoid the entanglements that may affect the company because of a member's bankruptcy, the operating agreement includes a springing option for the other members to purchase the bankrupt member's company interest for fair market value. The extent to which such a provision will be respected by a bankruptcy court is an open question that depends heavily on the facts and circumstances of the individual situation. Regardless of enforceability, the language of Article XIV is important to allow the members to seek to establish a presumption that they have an option to purchase the company interest of a bankrupt member, instead of simply relinquishing any claim to the company interest and permitting it to become part of the bankruptcy estate and subject to the third-party creditors of the bankrupt member.

ARTICLE XV

Dissolution and Termination of Company

1. **The Company shall be dissolved, the Company Assets shall be disposed of, and its affairs wound up, upon the earliest to occur of the following events:**

   (a) the prior written unanimous consent of the Managers and the Members, subject to Article X-3(d) hereof; or

   (b) at any time the Company has no Members for a period of ninety (90) consecutive days; or

   (c) the entry of a decree of judicial dissolution under §18-802 of the Act.

   Notwithstanding the foregoing or anything to the contrary contained in this Agreement and in furtherance of §18-801(a)(4) of the Act, the death, resignation, retirement, expulsion, termination or Bankruptcy of a Member, or other event of dissociation of a Member from the Company shall not constitute an event of dissolution of the Company.

The members can agree on any events of dissolution they choose. This can include specified dates of dissolution and other events the occurrence of which will require the dissolution of the company (e.g., the sale of a certain asset of the company, the completion of a specific project or achievement (or non-achievement) of a specified goal.)

> **2. The Company shall terminate when all the Company Assets have been disposed of (except for any liquid assets not so disposed of), and the net proceeds therefrom, as well as any other liquid or illiquid assets of the Company, shall, unless otherwise required by the Act, be distributed as follows: (i) first, to the creditors of the Company for the payment or due provisions for the liabilities of the Company (including loans, if any, to the Company from Members), and (ii) second, to the Class A Members and Class B Members, *pro rata*, in accordance with their respective positive Capital Account balances (after the allocation of all items of Profit, Loss, deduction, credit and deduction (or items thereof) under and pursuant to Article VII hereof).**

The dissolution of the company will effectively eliminate the personal liability shield the company provides to the members. Accordingly, the members should carefully consider the potential effects of dissolution before voting to dissolve. In many cases, the members are better served to simply allow the state registration of the company to lapse without dissolving, thereby eliminating the annual filings and upkeep related to the company, but preserving the ability of the members to reinstate the company as a liability shield.

> **3. Following the distribution of the net proceeds under Article XV-2 hereof and the completion of winding up the affairs of the Company, any Member, is hereby authorized and directed to have prepared and file a certificate of cancellation of the Company with the Office of the Secretary of**

State of Delaware, in accordance with §18-203 of
the Act, and take any and all other actions as may
be necessary and/or appropriate under the Act to
dissolve and terminate the Company.

ARTICLE XVI

Termination of Employment of a Member

The specifics of the following provision are taken from an operating
agreement prepared for one of our clients. The time frames, vesting
procedures, and percentages contained in this provision are arbitrary details
chosen by our client, and can be adjusted in any way for different
companies and scenarios. It is important to note that equity stakes in a
company should not be offered without a comprehensive understanding of
the economic and governance ramifications of the grant. The amount and
timing of an equity grant should be selected in a manner that properly
balances the incentive nature of the compensation and the upside sharing
with the expected economic benefit for the Class A members.

1. (a) Notwithstanding anything to the contrary
contained in this Agreement, including,
specifically, but without limitation, the
provisions of Article XIII-1 hereof, in the
event that a Class B Member's employment
terminates for any reason other than a
termination by the Company for Cause (as
defined below), the Company shall redeem
and liquidate all of the Class B Membership
Units owned by such Member (hereinafter
referred to as "Terminated Member") for a
redemption amount equal to the following:

   (i) if the terminating event occurs on or after
   the first (1st) anniversary of a Class B
   Member's starting date with the Company
   (the "First Anniversary Date"), but before
   the end of the first fiscal quarter
   thereafter, twenty-five percent (25%) of

the Fair Market Value of the Terminating Member's Class B Membership Units as of the date of such terminating event; and

(ii) an additional six and one quarter percent (6.25%) of the Fair Market Value of the Terminating Member's Class B Membership Units for each complete fiscal quarter following the First Anniversary Date that the Class B Member shall have been employed with the Company as of the date of the terminating event; provided, however, that no Class B Member shall be entitled to a redemption amount exceeding one hundred percent (100%) of the Fair Market Value of the Terminating Member's Class B Membership Units. As an example, if the terminating event occurs immediately after the start of the second quarter after the third (3rd) anniversary of a Terminated Member's starting date, the Company shall redeem and liquidate all of the Class B Membership Units owned by such Terminated Member for a redemption amount equal to eighty-one and one quarter percent (81.25%) of the Fair Market Value of the Terminating Member's Class B Membership Units as of the date of such terminating event (25% + (9 x 6.25%) = 81.25%).

The schedule in this agreement contemplates a four-year vesting period with no vesting in the first year, and then quarterly vesting thereafter. If a Class B member resigns or is terminated, other than a termination for cause, at any time after the first year, then the Class B units owned by that Class B member will be redeemed at a discount to the fair market value of the units.

(b) Notwithstanding anything to the contrary contained in this Agreement, if any time during the term of existence of the Company, the Terminating Member later participates, directly or indirectly, as an employee, consultant, independent contractor, officer, manager, owner, investor, director, stockholder, member, partner or otherwise have a financial interest in a Competing Business, then the payment terms of the redemption amount due to the Terminating Member shall be those set forth in Article XVI-2 and the Company shall have the right to offset any future payments of the redemption amount against any amounts still payable to the Terminating Member.

2. (a) In the event that a Class B Member's employment is terminated for Cause, the Company shall redeem and liquidate all of the Class B Membership Units owned by such Terminated Member for a redemption amount equal to fifty percent (50%) of the amount that such Terminated Member otherwise would have received pursuant to Article XVI-1 hereof. For purposes of this Article XVI, "Cause" means a termination of employment due to any of the following: (i) commission of a willful act of dishonesty in the course of such Member's duties hereunder, which is reasonably likely to cause material injury to the Corporation, (ii) conviction of such Member by a court of competent jurisdiction or a *nolo contendere* plea with respect to a crime constituting a felony, or conviction or a *nolo contendere* plea in respect of any act involving fraud, dishonesty or moral turpitude, (iii) performance by such Member under the influence of non-prescription controlled substances, or continued habitual intoxication, during working hours, (iv) material non-compliance with any of the policies and

> procedures of the Company, or (v) any breach of any material contractual obligations with the Company as set forth in any document including, without limitation, any employment agreement or binding offer letters by and between the Company and any employee of the Company.

A termination for "cause" results in a 50 percent reduction in the amount the Class B member would have otherwise received for his or her Class B units. "Cause" is a critical definition in any employment-type arrangement such as this one. We have provided a simple standard definition here, but "cause" can be expanded to cover any number of different scenarios and company concerns.

> (b) In the event that a Class B Member's employment is terminated for any reason other than for Cause, the Company shall have the option to redeem any and all Class B Units owned by such Class B Member for the Fair Market Value of any Company Interest redeemed pursuant to this Article XVI-2(b), subject to any restrictions placed on such Class B Units as set forth in Article XVI-1 hereof; it being understood and agreed that the determination to redeem any Class B Units pursuant to this Article XVI-2(b) shall be made in the sole and absolute discretion of the Managers.

> 3. In the event that a Class A Member's employment is terminated for Cause, the Company shall have the option to redeem any and all Class A Units owned by such Class A Member for the Fair Market Value of any Company Interest redeemed pursuant to this Article XVI-3; it being understood and agreed that the determination to redeem any Class A Units pursuant to this Article

XVI-3 shall be made in the sole and absolute
discretion of the Managers.

This agreement creates an option for the company to redeem Class A units
if a Class A member is terminated for cause. This is an atypical provision
that may not be acceptable to all Class A members who will be working for
the company. Please note, however, that the redemption of Class A units
under this Article XVI is for fair market value, without the discounts
applicable to Class B units.

4. **Settlement on the redemption and liquidation of
the Company Interests owned by the Terminated
Member under this Article XVI shall be held at
the principal office of the Company within ninety
(90) days following a terminating event. At
settlement on a redemption of the Company
Interests owned by the Terminated Member
under this Article XVI, the Terminated Member
(or his or her personal representatives) shall
execute and deliver (or cause to be executed and
delivered) to the Company an amendment to this
Agreement and any other documents, instruments
and agreements that the Company determines are
necessary and/or appropriate to reflect, among
other things, the complete redemption and
liquidation by the Company of the Company
Interests owned by the Terminated Member, the
withdrawal of the Terminated Member (and, if
applicable, any other owner of the Company
Interests owned by the Terminated Member) as a
Member and, if applicable, the resignation of the
Terminated Member as an Officer of the
Company, and the Company shall pay to the
Terminated Member twenty percent (20%) of the
Redemption Amount in immediately available
funds and, with respect to the remaining eighty
percent (80%), the Company shall execute and
deliver to the Terminated Member a promissory**

> note representing the balance of the purchase price payable in five (5) equal annual installments, together with accrued interest computed at an interest rate equal to the mid-term Applicable Federal Rate pursuant to Section 1274(d) of the I.R.C. in effect as of the date of such promissory note, beginning on the first (1st) anniversary of the date of settlement hereunder.

To avoid potential company cash flow issues, payment for the redemption of members under Article XVI is accomplished through a 20 percent initial payment, with the remainder payable pursuant to a promissory note. Generally, a form of the promissory note is attached to the equity incentive plan or equity grant agreement governing the grant of the Class B units to the Class B member.

> 5. In the event that the Company is sold (by way of merger, equity sale or asset sale, as the case may be), the Managers of the Company shall have the sole discretion to remove any restrictions, as set forth in Article XVI-1 hereof, placed on any or all of the Class B Membership Units and the Company shall have the option to redeem any and all of the Class B Membership Units for the Fair Market Value of such Class B Member's Company Interest represented by the number of Class B Membership Units redeemed pursuant to this Article XVI-5.

Article XVI-5 allows for accelerated vesting, at the option of the managers, in the event of a change in control transaction involving the company. This permits the managers to redeem all Class B units as part of a sale transaction, and prevents the Class B members from exercising outsize leverage in the negotiation of the terms of a sale.

> 6. Notwithstanding the provisions set forth in Article XVI hereof, the Managers of the Company may, in their sole and absolute discretion, waive any

restrictions, as set forth in Article XVI hereof or otherwise, placed on any or all of the Class B Membership Units granted to non-employees of the Company.

7. (a) If at any time a non-employee Class B Member ("Offered Non-Employee Member") receives a bona fide offer to purchase any or all of such Offered Non-Employee Member's Class B Membership Units (a "Third Party Offer") from a third party (an "Offeror"), which the Offered Non-Employee Member wishes to accept, the Offered Non-Employee Member shall cause the Third Party Offer to be reduced to writing and shall notify the Company in writing of its wish to accept the Third Party Offer. The Offered Non-Employee Member's notice to the Company shall contain an irrevocable offer to sell such Class B Membership Units to the Company (in the manner set forth below), and shall be accompanied by a copy of the Third Party Offer (which shall identify the Offeror). At any time within thirty (30) days after the date of the receipt by the Company of the Offered Non-Employee Member's notice, the Company shall have the right to elect, by delivery of notice to the Offered Non-Employee Member (an "Election Notice"), to redeem all or any portion of the Class B Membership Units covered by the Third Party Offer at the same price and on the same terms and conditions as the Third Party Offer (or, if the Third Party Offer includes any consideration other than cash, then at the sole option of the Company, at the equivalent all-cash price, determined in good faith by the Managers).

(b) The closing of any redemption, pursuant to Article XVI-7(a) hereof, shall occur within forty-five (45) days of delivery by the Company of its Election Notice (or such later time as is necessary to satisfy or obtain any regulatory approval) to the Offered Non-Employee Member. At the closing, the Company shall deliver a check or checks in the appropriate amount (or by wire transfer of immediately available funds, if the Offered Non-Employee Member provides to the Company wire transfer instructions) (and any such non-cash consideration to be paid) to the Offered Non-Employee Member against any instruments, if any, representing the Class B Membership Units so redeemed, appropriately endorsed by the Offered Non-Employee Member.

(c) If at the end of the thirty (30) day period referred to in Article XVI-7(a) hereof, the Company has not tendered an Election Notice to the Offered Non-Employee Member in the manner set forth above, the Offered Member may, during the succeeding sixty (60) day period, sell not less than all of the Class B Membership Units covered by the Third Party Offer, to the Offeror on terms no less favorable to the Offered Non-Employee Member than those contained in the Third Party Offer. Promptly after such sale, the Offered Non-Employee Member shall notify the Company of the consummation thereof and shall furnish such evidence of the completion and time of completion of such sale and of the terms thereof as may reasonably be requested by the Company. If, at the end of the sixty (60) day period referred to above, the Offered Non-Employee Member has not completed the sale of such Class B Membership Units as aforesaid,

> any and all of the restrictions on sale, transfer or assignment contained in this Agreement shall again be in effect with respect to such Class B Membership Units.

The provisions of XVI-7 implement a right of first refusal for the company in the event a Class B member is not redeemed at the time such Class B member's employment was terminated.

ARTICLE XVII

Confidentiality Provisions and Covenants Against Competition and Solicitation

A non-disclosure obligation is an essential component of an operating agreement, particularly when the company derives economic benefit from non-public, proprietary information, the disclosure of which could have an adverse effect on the company. In situations where one member is providing a significant amount of know-how to the company, there is a risk that, absent a non-disclosure covenant, other members may misappropriate the confidential information and use it for purposes other than the business of the company. Moreover, the company may develop important proprietary information in the course of its operations, and each member should be obligated to maintain the confidential nature of such information. Please note that the confidentiality provisions below require perpetual compliance and, unlike the non-compete obligations, are not time-limited.

1. Except as otherwise expressly permitted in writing by the Company, no Member (for purposes of this Article XVII, the term "Member" shall include any member, manager, partner, stockholder, officer or director of a Member hereof and, in the event that an entity is the Member shall:

    (a) use the Proprietary Information for any purpose other than the purpose for which the Company shared such information with such Member; or

(b) directly or indirectly copy, transfer, or otherwise disclose or reveal Proprietary Information to any person or entity other than the partners, employees, directors, officers, agents and consultants or a Member or Affiliate thereof who (i) have a need to know in connection with the relationship and/or discussions of the parties hereto, (ii) have been advised of such Proprietary Information's confidential status and (iii) are subject to legally binding obligations of confidentiality as to such Proprietary Information that are no less restrictive than those contained in this Agreement.

2. Each Member shall use at least the same degree (but no less than a reasonable degree) of care and protection to prevent the unauthorized use, dissemination or copying of any Proprietary Information as such Member uses to protect his, her or its own information of a like nature.

3. Each Member agrees not to assert any claim of title or ownership to the Proprietary Information or any portion thereof. If Proprietary Information consists of computer software disclosed in object code form, such Member shall not, and shall not permit any other party, to reverse engineer, reverse compile, or disassemble such object code, or take any other steps to derive a source code equivalent thereof.

4. If a Member becomes legally compelled (by depositions, interrogatory, subpoena, civil investigative demand or similar process) to disclose any Proprietary Information, he or she agrees to provide the Company with prompt prior written notice of such requirement so that the

Company may seek a protective order or other appropriate remedy. If such protective order or other remedy is not obtained, or if the Company waives, in writing, compliance with the terms hereof, such Member agrees to furnish only that portion of the Proprietary Information which he is advised by written opinion of his, her or its counsel is legally required, and to exercise reasonable efforts to obtain confidential treatment of such information.

5. Each Member hereby agrees that he or she shall destroy or return to the Company all copies of Proprietary Information promptly upon the earlier of (a) the Company's request at any time or (b) the termination of the membership in the Company of such Member.

6. During the period of time that a Member is a member of the Company and for two (2) years after such Member ceases to be a member, such Member shall not, with respect to the businesses described in Article XVII-7 hereof, directly or indirectly, whether as a proprietor, member, partner, stockholder, officer, consultant, independent contractor, co-venturer, employer, employee, agent, representative or in any other capacity, solicit business from, divert business from or perform services to or for any customer, client or account of the Company, including any customer, client or account over which such Member had responsibility or significant contact.

The enforceability of geographic and time limits on a member's, or former member's, participation in a competing business is a matter of state law. As a general matter, more stringent obligations are permissible with respect to a non-compete obligation that is coupled with an equity interest as compared with a non-compete obligation arising from employment alone.

When drafting non-compete provisions in operating agreements, the drafter should consider whether the applicable jurisdiction is a "blue pencil" state that will rewrite overly aggressive non-compete obligations to match state standards, or a state in which excessive non-compete obligations are vacated entirely. If the applicable jurisdiction is not a blue pencil state, then the drafter will need to be especially careful to research and comply with common law standards for non-compete obligations or risk creating a non-compete obligation that is not enforceable.

> 7. **During the period of time that a Member is a member of the Company and for two (2) years after such Member ceases to be a member, such Member shall not engage, directly or indirectly, in any Competing Business, whether as a proprietor, member, partner, stockholder, officer, consultant, independent contractor, co-venturer, employer, employee, agent, representative or in any other capacity, in any country or political subdivision in which the Company or any Affiliate conducts business or in any country or political subdivision of the world in which the Company or any Affiliate has, within the immediately preceding twelve (12) months, expressed an intention to conduct business.**

Please see our comments above.

> 8. **During the period of time that a Member is a member of the Company and for two (2) years after such Member ceases to be a member, such Member shall not directly or indirectly, whether as a proprietor, member, partner, stockholder, officer, consultant, independent contractor, co-venturer, employer, employee, agent, representative or in any other capacity, employ, recruit, solicit for employment, or for the purposes of hiring or engaging, any employee of the Company or any individual who was employed by the Company during the previous one (1)-year period.**

Please see our comments above.

9. If a Member shall violate any of the covenants or agreements under this Article XVII, the Company shall be entitled to an accounting and repayment of all gross profits, compensation, commissions, remunerations or benefits which such Member directly or indirectly realized and/or may realize as a result of, growing out of or in connection with any such violation; such remedy shall be in addition to and not in limitation of any injunctive relief or other rights or remedies to which the Company is or may be entitled at law or in equity or under this Agreement. The Company shall also be entitled to recover all costs and expenses, including, without limitation, reasonable fees of attorneys and paralegals that are incurred as a result of, growing out of or in connection with any such violation. Each party consents to personal jurisdiction in any such action brought in the State of Delaware and waives any objection or defense that such jurisdiction is invalid.

10. Each Member acknowledges that his, her or its agreement not to disclose Proprietary Information, as provided herein, is made as an inducement to the other parties hereto, to enter into this Agreement. Each Member and the Company have carefully read and considered the provisions of this Article XVII and, having done so, agree that the restrictions set forth in such sections are fair and reasonable and are reasonably required for the protection of the interests of the Company, any Affiliate, and the respective members, partners, stockholders, officers, directors and employees of the same.

11. Each Member shall disclose promptly to the Company and any Affiliate any and all significant

conceptions and ideas for inventions, improvements, and valuable discoveries, whether patentable or not, that are conceived or made by such Member, solely or jointly with another, as a result of his, her or its exposure to Proprietary Information or his, her or its membership in, or management of, the Company, and that the Company views as directly related to the business or activities of the Company or any Affiliate, regardless of whether or not such ideas, inventions or improvements qualify as "works for hire." Each Member hereby assigns and agrees to assign all his, her or its interests in such ideas, inventions or improvements to the Company. Whenever requested to do so by the Company, such Member shall execute any and all applications, assignments or other instruments that the Company shall deem necessary to apply for and obtain Letters Patent of the United States or any foreign country or to otherwise protect the Company's interest therein.

12. Each Member shall disclose promptly to the Company and any Affiliate any and all significant works, and any and all derivative works thereof, that are created by such Member as a result of his, her or its exposure to Proprietary Information or his, her or its membership in, or management of, the Company, solely or jointly with another, and that the Company reasonably views as directly related to the business or activities of the Company or any Affiliate, regardless of whether such works qualify as "works for hire." Each Member hereby assigns and agrees to assign all his, her or its interests in such works to the Company. Whenever requested to do so by the Company, each Member shall take all actions and cooperate as is necessary to protect the copyrightability of the works and further agrees to

> execute any documents that might be necessary
> to perfect the Company's ownership of copyrights
> in such works including registration thereof.

Increasingly, a significant portion of the value of a business, particularly small businesses, is the intellectual property created by the company and its employees. To preserve this value, the company must be able to control the intellectual property created by its employees and members. The provisions of Article XVII (12) seek to characterize all intellectual property created by a member as a "work made for hire," which vests the company with ownership of the intellectual property without the need to document an assignment of intellectual property from the member to the company.

> 13. If any provision or part of any provision of this
>   Agreement shall for any reason be held invalid,
>   illegal or unenforceable in any respect, the
>   remaining provisions and remaining parts of
>   provisions, as the case may be, shall be construed
>   as if such invalid, illegal or unenforceable
>   provision or part of a provision had never been
>   contained herein. Further, in the event that a
>   court declares that the imposition of a time period
>   and/or an area of restriction is reasonable or
>   needs to be adjusted for purposes of the
>   enforceability of this Agreement, then this
>   Agreement shall be appropriately modified so that
>   such time period and/or area of restriction shall
>   be deemed to be part of this Agreement.

ARTICLE XVIII

Miscellaneous Provisions

Article XVIII contains the typical administrative provisions contained in an operating agreement. Despite their status as "legal boilerplate," the following provisions contain important concepts and tools that will increase the enforceability and ease of interpretation of the agreement and should not be overlooked when drafting.

1. The Members hereby agree to execute and deliver all documents (subject to the provisions of Article XVII-5), provide all information and take or refrain from all such action as may be reasonably necessary or appropriate to achieve the purposes of this Agreement and the Certificate.

2. Except as expressly provided in this Agreement, nothing contained herein shall be construed to constitute any Member the agent of any other Member hereof or to limit in any manner the Members in the carrying on of their own respective businesses or activities. Each Member may engage in and/or possess any interest in other business ventures of every nature and description, independently or with others, whether existing as of the date hereof or hereafter coming into existence; and neither the Company nor any Member hereof shall have any rights in or to any such independent ventures or the income or profits derived therefrom.

3. Unless otherwise provided herein, the Managers and Members hereby agree that, in connection with any dispute between or among the Managers and/or the Members with respect to any decision to be made or action to be taken, the parties shall, for thirty (30) days from the date such dispute arises, use good faith efforts to resolve such dispute in the best interests of the Company. In furtherance of the foregoing, it is understood and agreed by and among the parties hereto that, upon the expiration of such thirty (30)-day period, any such claim or controversy shall, upon the request of any party (or parties) involved, be submitted to and settled by non-binding mediation. In the event that the parties fail to resolve such claim or controversy through non-

binding mediation and as a condition precedent to any litigation with respect to any claim or controversy arising out of or relating to this Agreement (or a breach hereof) and/or the Company, then the parties shall submit the claim or controversy to binding arbitration, in which event the resolution of the claim or controversy shall be made in accordance with the rules, regulations and procedures of the American Arbitration Association (as applicable in the State of Delaware). The resolution of any claim or controversy by binding arbitration hereunder shall be final, binding and conclusive upon the Company, the Managers and the Members.

4. (a) All notices provided for herein shall be in writing, hand-delivered, with receipt therefor, or sent by certified or registered mail, return receipt requested, and first-class postage prepaid, or by overnight courier, to the address of each Member as shown in Exhibit A, unless notice of a change of address is given to the Company pursuant to the provisions of this Article XVIII-4. Any notice which is required to be given within a stated period of time shall be considered timely if delivered or postmarked before midnight of the last day of such period. Any notice made hereunder shall be deemed effective for all purposes and in all respects when sent (or given) to any Member at the address set forth in Exhibit A hereof, or at such other address specified by a Member for which notice has been received by the Company in accordance with this Article XVIII-4.

(b) Where the consent or approval of any Member is required by this Agreement, the failure of such Member to respond (either affirmatively or negatively) in writing after the Company has sent two (2) notices requesting such approval to such Member, with the second such notice being sent by the Company at least ten (10) days following the first such notice, then, after the expiration of ten (10) days following the date the second such notice was sent, such failure to respond shall be conclusively deemed the affirmative consent or approval of such Member.

5. Any and all amendments to this Agreement shall require the affirmative vote of the majority-in-Membership Units of the Class A Members; *provided, however,* that any and all amendments to this Agreement that will adversely affect any substantive right of a Class A Member shall require the unanimous vote of the Membership Units of the Class A Members.

6. By executing this Agreement, each Member (who is not otherwise a Manager) irrevocably makes, constitutes and appoints the Managers as such Member's true and lawful attorney-in-fact and agent with full power and authority in his, her or its name, place and stead to make, execute, sign, acknowledge, deliver, file and record with respect to the Company the following:

   (a) All amendments to this Agreement and/or the Certificate and all other instruments and documents which the Managers deem appropriate to qualify or to continue the Company as a limited liability company in each jurisdiction in which the Company conducts business;

(b) All instruments which the Managers deem appropriate to reflect (i) any change or modification of the terms and conditions governing the relationship among the Members and the Company or (ii) an amendment of this Agreement and/or the Certificate, made in accordance with this Agreement;

(c) All conveyances and other instruments, certificates or documents which the Managers deem appropriate to effect, evidence and/or reflect any sales or transfers by, or the dissolution, termination and/or liquidation of, the Company, including any sales or transfer of Company Interests pursuant to this Agreement;

(d) All such other instruments, documents and certificates which may from time to time be required by the Company, its lenders, the Internal Revenue Service, the State of Delaware, the United States of America, or any political subdivision within which the Company conducts its business, to effectuate, implement, continue and defend the valid and continuing existence of the Company as a limited liability company and to carry out the intention and purpose of this Agreement; and

(e) All amendments to this Agreement and any other documents, instruments and certificates which may be required to admit additional Members or Substituted Members. If a Member assigns its Company Interest under and pursuant to Article XIII or XIV hereof, the foregoing power of attorney shall survive the delivery of the instruments effecting such assignment for the purpose of enabling the Managers to sign, swear to, execute, acknowledge and file any amendments to the Certificate and other instruments and documents in order to effectuate the substitution of the assignee as a Member. It is expressly intended that the foregoing power of attorney under this Article XVIII-5 is a durable power of attorney which shall not be affected by the subsequent physical or mental disability or incapacity of a Member, and such power of attorney is coupled with an interest; provided, however, that the Managers shall not exercise the same in any manner which would (i) remove a Manager, (ii) enlarge any obligation or liability of a Member, or (iii) affect any Company distributions in a manner materially adverse to any Member, except to the extent any Member adversely affected thereby has previously consented thereto in writing.

This attorney-in-fact provision is intended for the managers' administrative convenience and is generally included in all of our operating agreements. Its purpose is simply to streamline the ability of the managers to effect those actions that have been properly authorized under the operating agreement, and does not permit the managers to act outside the scope of the authority already granted therein.

7. This Agreement and the rights of the parties hereunder will be governed by, interpreted and enforced in accordance with the laws of the State of Delaware, without regard to principles of conflicts of laws or choice of law.

8. This Agreement shall inure to the benefit of and bind the parties hereto, and their respective members, managers, partners, legal representatives, successors and, subject to the provisions of Article XIII hereof, assigns.

9. This Agreement, together with Exhibit A attached hereto, and the Certificate set forth and are intended by all parties hereto to be an integration of all of the promises, agreements, conditions, understandings, warranties and representations between the parties hereto with respect to the Company, the Company's business and the Company Assets, and there are no promises, agreements, conditions, understandings, warranties or representations, oral or written, express or implied, except as set forth herein.

10. If any provision of this Agreement is held to be illegal, invalid or unenforceable under the present or future laws effective during the term of this Agreement, such provision will be fully severable; this Agreement will be construed and enforced as if such illegal, invalid or unenforceable provision had never comprised a part of this Agreement; and the remaining provisions of this Agreement will remain in full force and effect and will not be affected by the illegal, invalid or unenforceable provision or by its severance from this Agreement.

11. This Agreement is made solely and specifically among and for the benefit of the parties hereto, and their respective successors and assigns, subject to the express provisions hereof relating to successors and assigns, and no other Person will have any rights, interest or claims hereunder or be entitled to any benefits under or on account of this Agreement as a third party beneficiary or otherwise. In furtherance of and not in limitation of the foregoing, nothing contained in this Agreement is intended to be for the benefit of any creditor or other Person (other than a Member in his, her or its capacity as a member of the Company) to whom or which any debts, liabilities

or obligations are owed by the Company or any of the Members; and no such creditor or other Person shall obtain any right hereunder against the Company or any of the Members by reason of any debt, liability or obligation (or otherwise).

12. This Agreement may be executed in several counterparts, each of which will be deemed an original but all of which together will constitute one and the same instrument.

{Signatures appear on the following page.}

The undersigned parties have executed this Limited Liability Company Agreement as of the date first above written.

WITNESS   MEMBERS:

                                 [_____]

_____   By: _____
                                 [_____]

_____   _____
                                 [_____]

_____   _____
                                 [_____]

EXHIBIT A
TO
LIMITED LIABILITY COMPANY AGREEMENT
OF
NEWCO, LLC

Class A Members:	Contributions	Percentage Capital Company Interest
[_____]	[_____]	[_____]
[_____]	[_____]	[_____]
[_____]	[_____]	[_____]
	_____	_____
Totals	[_____]	100.0%

Class B Members

None

Appendix:
Sample LLC Operating Agreement

LIMITED LIABILITY COMPANY AGREEMENT
OF
NEWCO, LLC

July 1, 2012

LIMITED LIABILITY COMPANY AGREEMENT
OF
NEWCO, LLC

THIS LIMITED LIABILITY COMPANY AGREEMENT is made and entered into, effective for all purposes and in all respects as of the 1st day of July, 2012, by and among the undersigned parties.

WHEREAS, certain undersigned parties have formed (or caused to be formed) a limited liability company known as "Newco, LLC" (the "Company," as defined herein), for the purposes set forth in Article IV hereof, pursuant to the "Act" (as defined herein) and other relevant laws of the State of Delaware; and

WHEREAS, the undersigned parties desire to set forth herein their agreements and understandings with respect to the ownership and operation of the Company.

NOW, THEREFORE, in consideration of the foregoing and other good and valuable consideration, the receipt and sufficiency of which are hereby acknowledged, the undersigned parties, intending legally and equitably to be bound, hereby covenant and agree as follows:

ARTICLE I

Definitions

1. The following terms shall have the indicated meanings ascribed to them when used herein:

"Act" shall mean and refer to the Delaware Limited Liability Company Act [Delaware Code Annotated, Title 6, §§18-101 *et seq.* (1992)].

"Additional Capital Contributions" shall mean and refer to any additional cash Capital Contributions made by a Member to the Company in order to fund any Additional Funds under Article VI-2 hereof, *reduced by* distributions to such Member pursuant to Article XII-1 hereof.

"Additional Funds" shall have the meaning ascribed to such term in Article VI-2 hereof.

"Affiliate" shall mean, as to any Person, any other Person controlled by, controlling or under common control with such Person, and "control" means the power to manage or direct the affairs of the Person in question, whether by ownership of voting securities, by contract, or otherwise.

"Agreement" shall mean and refer to this Limited Liability Company Agreement and Exhibit A attached hereto, as originally executed and as amended from time to time in writing.

"Bankruptcy" (and any derivations thereof) shall mean and refer to an adjudication of bankruptcy under Title 11 of the United States Code, as amended, an assignment for the benefit of creditors and/or an adjudication of insolvency under any state or local insolvency statute or procedure or the occurrence of any other event of bankruptcy or insolvency under the Act.

"Capital Account" shall, with respect to each Member, mean and refer to the separate "book" account for such Member to be established and maintained in all events in the manner provided under, and in accordance with, Treasury Regulation §1.704-1(b)(2)(iv), as amended, and in accordance with the other provisions of Treasury Regulation §1.704-1(b) that must be complied with in order for the Capital Accounts to be determined and maintained in accordance with the provisions of Treasury Regulation §1.704-1(b)(2)(iv). In furtherance of and consistent with the foregoing, a Member's Capital Account shall include generally, without limitation, the Capital Contributions of such Member (as of any particular date), (i) increased by such Member's distributive share of Profit of the Company (including, if such date is not the close of the Company Accounting Year, the distributive share of Profit of the Company for the period from the close of the last Company Accounting Year to such date), and (ii) decreased by such Member's distributive share of Loss of the Company and distributions by the Company to such Member (including, if such date is not the close of the Company Accounting Year, the distributive share of Loss of the Company and distributions by the Company during the period from the close of the last Company Accounting Year to such date). For purposes of the foregoing, distributions of property shall result in a decrease in a Member's Capital

Account equal to the agreed fair market value of such property distributed (less the amount of indebtedness, if any, of the Company which is assumed by such Member and/or the amount of indebtedness, if any, to which such property is subject, as of the date of distribution) by the Company to such Member.

"Capital Contribution" or "Capital Contributions" shall mean and refer to the amount of cash and/or the agreed fair market value of property [less the amount of indebtedness, if any, of a Member which is assumed by the Company and/or the amount of indebtedness, if any, to which such property is subject, as of the date of contribution (without regard to the provisions of I.R.C. Section 7701(g))] actually contributed by a Member to the capital of the Company, including, but not limited to, any amounts paid by a Member (except to the extent indemnification is made by another Member) in respect of any claims, liabilities or obligations against the Company and/or pursuant to any guaranty of Company indebtedness or otherwise by such Member.

"Certificate" shall mean and refer to that certain Certificate of Formation of the Company filed with, and approved by, the Office of the Secretary of State of Delaware, as the same may be amended, modified, supplemented and/or restated from time to time.

"Class A Member" or "Class A Members" shall mean and refer to that Person or those Persons designated as such in Exhibit A.

"Class A Membership Units" shall mean and refer to Membership Units granted or assigned to a Class A Member or Class A Members.

"Class B Member" or "Class B Members" shall mean and refer to that Person or those Persons designated as such in Exhibit A.

"Class B Membership Units" shall mean and refer to Membership Units granted to a Class B Member or Class B Members.

"Company" shall mean and refer to Newco, LLC, a Delaware limited liability company formed under and pursuant to the Act and other relevant laws of the State of Delaware and owned and operated pursuant to the terms of this Agreement.

"Company Accounting Year" shall mean and refer to the twelve (12)-month period ending December 31 of each year, which shall constitute the accounting year of the Company, or any shorter period applicable hereunder.

"Company Assets" at any particular time, shall mean and refer to all property and assets (tangible or intangible, choate or inchoate, fixed or contingent) which the Company may own, hold, acquire, operate and/or manage from time to time, as such assets are more fully described on the books and records of the Company.

"Company Interest", as to any Member, shall mean and refer to the entire ownership interest of such Member in the Company at any particular time, including such Member's Capital Account, Membership Units, right to distributions under Article XII-1 hereof and the right of such Member to any and all benefits to which a Member may be entitled as provided in this Agreement and under the Act, together with the obligations of such Member to comply with all of the terms and provisions of this Agreement and the Act.

"Competing Business" shall mean and refer to (1) any business that is similar or related to the business of the Company, or (2) the rendering of services that are the same or substantially the same as the services, if any, rendered by such Member on behalf of the Company.

"Exhibit A" shall mean and refer to the original Exhibit A to this Agreement, relating to the names and addresses of the Class A Members and the Class B Members, as may be amended from time to time.

"Fair Market Value" of a Company Interest shall be determined based on the price which would be paid by a willing buyer to a willing seller in an arms'-length transaction for the purchase of such Company Interest, free and clear of any option, call, contract, commitment, demand, lien, charge, security interest or encumbrance of any kind whatsoever, as such price may be mutually determined by the interested Members (or groups of interested Members) and the Company (as applicable), or, if the interested Members (or groups of interested Members) and the Company (as applicable) cannot mutually agree upon such price within fifteen (15) days after the event triggering a determination of Fair Market Value, the Fair Market Value of such Company Interest shall be determined as follows: The interested parties shall agree on a single appraiser within thirty (30) days after the expiration of the fifteen (15)-day period above or, if the interested parties are unable to agree on a single appraiser, then each interested Member (or group of interested Members) and the Company (as applicable) shall promptly appoint an appraiser, who or which shall determine mutually the Fair Market Value of such Company Interest, for purposes of an all-cash sale. All appraisers appointed hereunder shall be directed to take into account any "minority ownership discounts," "lack of marketability discounts" and/or other applicable valuation discounts in valuing such Company Interest. If the two (2) appraisers agree upon the fair market value of the Company Interest, they shall jointly render a single written report of their opinion thereon; provided, however, that, if the two (2) appraisers cannot agree upon the fair market value of the Company Interest and their respective appraisals are within ten percent (10%) of each other, then the Fair Market Value shall be the average of the two (2) appraisals; and provided, further that if the two (2) appraisers cannot agree upon the fair market value of the Company Interest and their respective appraisals are not within ten percent (10%) of each other, then they shall together appoint a third (3rd) appraiser, who or which shall determine the Fair Market Value of such Company Interest, and shall send written notice of such determination to each Member. All appraisers appointed shall be duly licensed and qualified by experience and ability to value entities similar to the Company; and the fees and other costs of each of the first two (2) appraisers shall be borne by the Member (or group of Members) or the Company (as applicable) appointing each such appraiser, with the fees and other costs of the third (3rd) appraiser (if applicable) being shared equally by the Company and the Members (or group of Members). The Fair Market Value determined by the first two (2) appraisers or the third (3rd) appraiser (as the case may be) shall be used to determine the purchase price of the Company Interest; provided, however, that, if the Fair Market Value determined by the third (3rd) appraiser is more than the higher of the first two (2) appraisers, the higher determination of the first two (2) appraisers shall govern; and provided, further, that if the Fair Market Value determined by the third (3rd) appraiser is less than the lower determination of the first two (2) appraisers, the lower determination of the first two (2) appraisers shall govern.

"Indemnified Party" shall have the meaning ascribed to such term in Article X-9(a) hereof.

"I.R.C." shall mean and refer to the Internal Revenue Code of 1986, as amended, or any similar Federal internal revenue law enacted in substitution of the Internal Revenue Code of 1986, and the corresponding revenue law (and sections thereof) of any state or jurisdiction.

"Loss" shall have the meaning ascribed to such term in Article VII-1 hereof.

"Manager" or "Managers" shall mean and refer initially to [_____], and [_____], subject to the provisions of Article X-2 hereof.

"Member" or "Members" shall mean and refer to the Class A Members and the Class B Members designated as such in Exhibit A.

"Membership Unit" and "Membership Units" shall mean and refer to the One Hundred (100) Membership Units of membership interest in the Company which the Company is authorized to issue. Each Membership Unit shall represent an undivided membership interest as a Member in the Company.

"Net Capital Investment" shall, with respect to each Member, mean and refer to the cash Capital Contributions by such Member to the Company, excluding any Additional Capital Contributions by such Member, *reduced by* any distributions to such Member pursuant to Article XII-1 hereof.

"Net Cash Flow" shall mean and refer to the total cash receipts of the Company (including, without limitation, any loan proceeds, gross sales proceeds and operating revenues, but excluding Capital Contributions), *plus* any other funds (including amounts previously set aside as reserves by the Managers, where and to the extent the Managers no longer regard such reserves as reasonably necessary in the efficient conduct and/or expansion of the Company business) deemed available for distribution and designated as "Net Cash Flow" by the Managers, in their sole discretion, *less* the total cash disbursements of the Company such as, but not limited to, the salaries and other compensation paid to any employees of the Company, other operating expenses of the Company and repayments of any loans made to the Company by any Person whatsoever (including loans from any Member and/or any Affiliate thereof), *less* such reserves or other uses of cash as the Managers, in their sole discretion, shall deem to be necessary for the efficient conduct of the Company business, including the purchase of additional Company Assets.

"Officer" or "Officers" shall mean and refer to that person or those persons appointed by the Managers to serve as (an) executive officer(s) of the Company, which person or persons shall have the right, power and authority to manage and oversee the day-to-day business and operations of the Company, as more fully set forth in Article X-2 hereof.

"Percentage Interest" of a Member shall mean and refer to the percentage participation in the Company of such Member.

"Permitted Transferee" of a Member shall mean and refer to any of the following: (i) such Member's spouse or natural or adopted descendant or descendants, (ii) any Person already a Member, (iii) a trust, whether *inter vivos* or testamentary, in which any person or entity named in (i) or (ii) above is the primary income beneficiary, (iv) a family limited partnership or family limited liability company formed by a Member, in which the sole partners or members (as the case may be) are such Member and/or his Affiliates, or (v) in the case of a Member which is a trust, to any beneficiaries of such trust.

"Person" shall mean and refer to an individual or entity, such as, but not limited to, a corporation, general partnership, joint venture, limited partnership, limited liability company, trust, foundation or business association.

"Preferred Return" shall, with respect to any Class A Member, mean and refer to an aggregate amount equal to (i) a twelve percent (12%) *per annum*, cumulative but noncompounded, on such Class A Member's respective Net Capital Investment, as computed and aggregated on a *per diem* basis for each Company Accounting Year comments as of the date such Class A Member makes (or is deemed to have made) Capital Contributions to the Company, *less* (ii) any distributions actually made to such Class A Member under Article XII-2(a) hereof.

"Prime Rate" shall mean and refer to the "prime rate" offered by U.S. banks as published from time to time in the "Money Rates" section of *The Wall Street Journal.*

"Profit" shall have the meaning ascribed to such term in Article VII-1 hereof.

"Proprietary Information" shall mean any confidential, proprietary and/or trade secret information concerning the Company's products, technology, services, finances, personnel or business methods, practices or policies, including, without limitation, information relating to research and development, know-how, inventions, specifications, software, market analysis, research strategies, projections and forecasts, except to the extent to which a Member can establish by legally sufficient evidence that such information: (i) was rightfully in such Member's possession before receipt from the Company; (ii) is or becomes a matter of public knowledge through no fault of such Member; (iii) is rightfully received by such Member from a third party without violation of any duty of confidentiality; or (iv) is or was independently developed by or for such Member. Subject to the foregoing exceptions, "Proprietary Information" also includes, without limitation, (x) information of a similar nature received by the Company from third parties that the Company is obligated to treat as confidential, and information in combination with publicly known information where the nature of the combination is not publicly known and (y) the same or similar type of information of any Affiliate, regardless of whether the Company transfers this Agreement to any such Affiliate. However, "Proprietary Information" shall not include information regarding a product, service or technology that the Company has determined, in writing, that it will not pursue for commercial exploitation.

"Substituted Member" or "Substituted Members" shall mean and refer to that Person or those Persons admitted to the Company as a Member or Members, in accordance with the provisions of Article XIII hereof and so reflected in Exhibit A attached hereto.

"Tax Liability" shall, with respect to each Member, mean an amount equal to the Federal and state income tax liability attributable to any income or gain allocated to such Member by the Company. The Tax Liability shall be equal to the maximum Federal and state income tax rates (based on the state with the highest income tax rate among all the states where the Members reside) that apply to ordinary income or long-term capital gain, as applicable; it being understood and agreed that the Managers may, in their reasonable discretion, take into account Losses from prior Company

Accounting Years attributable to a Member and not used by such Member due to at-risk limitations under I.R.C. Section 105 in determining the amount of a Member's Tax Liability to be distributed to a Member.

"Tax Matters Partner" shall have the meaning ascribed to such term in Article X-6(a) hereof.

"Withdrawal Event" shall have the meaing set forth in Article X-2(b) hereof.

2. Unless the context clearly indicates otherwise, where appropriate the singular shall include the plural and any pronoun shall include the masculine, feminine and neuter, to the extent necessary to give the terms defined in this Article I and/or the terms otherwise used in this Agreement their proper meanings.

3. Unless specifically and expressly limited in the context, any reference herein to a decision, determination, act, action, exercise of a right, power or privilege, or other procedure by the Managers shall mean and refer to such decision, determination, act, action, exercise or other procedure of the Managers, in their reasonable discretion.

ARTICLE II

Name of Company

The name of the Company shall be "Newco, LLC."

ARTICLE III

Term of Company; Formation

1. The Company shall have perpetual existence, unless sooner terminated in accordance with the provisions of Article XV hereof.

2. The undersigned Members heretofore authorized [Law Firm] to act as organizer in order to form the Company under and pursuant to the Act by filing the Certificate on behalf of themselves and any additional or Substituted Members. This Agreement is subject to, and governed by,

the Act. In the event of a direct conflict between the provisions of this Agreement and the mandatory provisions of the Act, such mandatory provisions of the Act shall be controlling. The Company shall have perpetual existence, unless sooner terminated in accordance with the provisions of Article XV.

ARTICLE IV

Business of Company

The general purposes and business objectives of the Company are to [_____].

ARTICLE V

Principal Office; Registered Office and Registered Agent

The principal office of the Company shall be located at [_____]. The Managers may change the principal office of the Company and/or establish additional offices of the Company, either within or without the State of Delaware, as the Managers may deem advisable. The registered office of the Company shall be located at [_____]. The registered agent of the Company in the State of Delaware for service of process shall be [_____], which is a Delaware corporation. The Managers may, in their sole and absolute discretion, change the registered agent of the Company to a Person who or which qualifies as a registered agent under the Act.

ARTICLE VI

Capital Contributions; Membership Units

1. (a) The Company shall issue to each of the Class A Members a number of Membership Units proportionate to each Class A Member's respective Capital Contribution. The Class A Members (in their capacity as Class A Members), have committed to make an aggregate Capital Contribution to the Company, as indicated on Exhibit A, attached hereto.

(b) (i) None of the Class B Members shall be required to make any Capital Contribution to the Company. Simultaneously with the execution of this Agreement, the Company shall issue to each Class B Member the number of Membership Units set forth in a separate letter to each of the Class B Members.

(ii) Notwithstanding anything to the contrary contained herein, the Company Interest granted to each of the Class B Members is a "profits interest" pursuant to, and in accordance with, Rev. Proc. 93-27 (1992-2 CB 343) and Rev. Proc. 2001-43 (2001-34 IRB 191) (the "Revenue Procedures"). Such Company Interest has been granted to each of the Class B Members in exchange for the provision of services by each such Class B Member for, and on behalf of, the Company. Moreover, the Class B Members' Company Interests granted hereby do not entitle the Class B Members as of the date hereof to a share of the proceeds if the Company Assets were sold at Fair Market Value and such proceeds were distributed in complete liquidation of the Company. Each of the Class B Members hereby agrees to take into account the distributive share of partnership income, gain, loss, deduction and credit associated with such Company Interests in computing his, her or its income tax liability for the entire period during which such Class B Member owns his, her or its Company Interest.

(iii) In accordance with the Revenue Procedures, the grant of the Company Interest to the Class B Members hereby is not a taxable event.

2. (a) In the event that at any time (or from time to time) the Managers determine (in their reasonable discretion) that additional funds are required by the Company for or in respect of its business or any of its obligations, expenses, costs, liabilities or expenditures (the "Additional Funds"), then the Managers, acting for and on behalf of, and in the name of, the Company, in the exercise of their reasonable discretion and in furtherance of the provisions of Article X-1 hereof, may cause the Company to borrow the Additional funds, with interest payable at then-prevailing rates, from commercial banks,

savings and loan associations and/or other lending institutions or from any other Persons, including the Members or Affiliates thereof. In the event that the Company seeks any Additional Funds by way of a loan from a Member, it shall offer such opportunity to all members, *pro rata* in proportion to their respective Percentage Interests (unless Members participating in making any such loan shall agree upon any other ratio).

(b) Notwithstanding any provision to the contrary contained in this Agreement, in the event that the Managers are unable or unwilling to cause the Company to borrow the Additional Funds in accordance with the provisions of Article VI-2(a) above, then the Managers, acting for and on behalf of, and in the name of, the Company and in accordance with the provisions of Article X hereof, shall send written notice thereof to each of the Members (a "Call Notice"), which shall set forth the amount of Capital Contributions required, and the Members, *pro rata*, in proportion to their respective Percentage Interests (unless they unanimously agree upon another proportion), shall (and hereby covenant and agree to) contribute such Capital Contributions to the Company within ten (10) business days of the Call Notice (the "Contribution Period"); it being understood and agreed that all such required Additional Funds may be treated as a Capital Contribution and/or loans uniformly, as determined by the Managers, in their sole and absolute discretion.

(c) (i) Notwithstanding any provision contained in this Agreement, in the event that any Member (such Member, hereinafter in this Article VI-2(c), being referred to as the "Defaulting Member") fails to contribute to the Company his proportionate share of the Capital Contributions required under the Call Notice prior to the expiration of the Contribution Period, then each non-Defaulting Member may (but need not) fund such non-Defaulting Member's proportionate share of the defaulted Capital Contribution by way of a Default Loan (as defined below) to or for the benefit of the Defaulting Member.

(ii) If a non-Defaulting Member chooses to fund his proportionate share of the defaulted Capital Contribution by way of a loan, such non-Defaulting Member shall make a Capital Contribution to the Company for the benefit of (and credited to the Capital Account of) the Defaulting Member equal to the principal amount of such loan, which loan shall constitute a recourse advance (a "Default Loan") to the Defaulting Member, the principal of which shall be repayable on or before ninety (90) days from the date of such advance, together with interest thereon at the lesser of (x) an annual rate, compounded quarterly, equal to two (2) times the Prime Rate as of the date of the advance, and (y) the maximum rate permitted by law, and secured, *pro rata* with all other such loans with respect to any such defaulted Capital Contribution, by the Defaulting Member's Company Interest (including any distributions otherwise payable to the Defaulting Member).

(iii) In the event that a Defaulting Member fails to repay all amounts owed with respect to a Default Loan in accordance with Article VI-2(c)(ii) above, time being of the essence, then each non-Defaulting Member that made a Default Loan to the Defaulting Member may elect to purchase a portion of the Defaulting Member's Company Interest by applying all amounts owed by the Defaulting Member with respect to the Default Loan to the purchase price for a portion of the Company Interest theretofore owned by the Defaulting Member. The portion of the Defaulting Member's Company Interest to be purchased as a result of the foregoing shall be equal to the product of (A) the Company Interest of the Defaulting Member, and (B) a fraction, the numerator of which is the dollar amount of the amounts owed by the Defaulting Member to the non-Defaulting Member with respect to the Default Loan, and the denominator of which is the sum of all Capital Contributions of the Defaulting Member plus the Defaulting Member's portion of the Additional Funds that had been called for by the Company through the Call Notice giving rise to such default (whether or not paid in).

(iv) Each Member hereby unconditionally and irrevocably grants to the Company a security interest in such Member's Company

Interest to secure such Member's obligation to repay timely any Default Loans deemed made to it pursuant to Article VI-2(c)(ii). The Company shall assign to those non-Defaulting Members making such Default Loans, ratably in proportion to the principal amounts of each such Default Loan, its security interest in a Defaulting Member's Company Interest in order to secure such Default Loans. This Agreement shall be deemed to be a security and pledge agreement in respect of such grant.

(v) To the extent that any portion of a defaulted Capital Contribution is not so funded by non-Defaulting Members, the Defaulting Member shall remain fully liable to the Company to the extent thereof, plus interest at the lesser of (x) an annual rate, compounded quarterly, equal to two (2) times the Prime Rate as of the date of the advance, and (y) the maximum rate permitted by law, from the date of the default to (but not including) the date of payment.

(vi) Except as otherwise provided herein, no right, power or remedy conferred upon the Company in this Article VI-2(c) shall be exclusive, and each such right, power, or remedy shall be cumulative and in addition to every other right, power or remedy, whether conferred in this Article VI-2(c) or now or hereafter available at law or in equity or by statute or otherwise. No course of dealing between the Company and any Defaulting Member and no delay in exercising any right, power or remedy shall operate as a waiver or otherwise prejudice any such right, power or remedy. The Defaulting Member shall be liable for all expenses and costs (including reasonable attorneys' and other professionals' fees and disbursements) incurred by the Company, the Managers or any non-Defaulting Member in enforcing any of the remedies or rights set forth in this Article VI-2(c). The Company may bring an action against the Defaulting Member to enforce payment of the defaulted Capital Contribution and interest thereon, as well as the payment of all costs and expenses of collection. Each Member acknowledges by its execution of this Agreement that it has been admitted to the Company in reliance upon its agreements that the Company and each other Member may have and exercise any and all rights, powers and remedies provided for in this Article VI-2(c) or otherwise available at law or in equity, and furthermore specifically acknowledges and agrees that, notwithstanding anything to the contrary in this Agreement, the Company shall have the right and power to take such other action as the Managers may deem reasonably necessary or advisable to protect the interests of the Company and the other Members upon a Member's default.

(d) Until such time as the outstanding amount of any Default Loan, together with accrued interest at the aforesaid rate, is repaid in full to the non-Defaulting Member(s), any and all amounts otherwise distributable to the Defaulting Member (or his permitted assigns) under this Agreement (including, without limitation, distributions of Net Cash Flow under Article XII hereof) shall be distributed by the Company to the non-Defaulting Member in satisfaction (in whole or in part) of the Default Loan (the "Designated Distributions").

3. Notwithstanding anything to the contrary contained in this Agreement or under the Act, any issuance of additional Membership Units, other than to employees of the Company in consideration of their services, shall be subject to the following preemptive rights: Each Class A Member shall have the right (but not the obligation) to purchase a portion of any additional Membership Units so issued that is proportionate to such Class A Member's percentage ownership of Class A Membership Units at the same price, time and terms as for any other Person. If any additional Membership Units are issued, directly or indirectly, to [_____] (each an "Existing Class A Member"), such Existing Class A Member shall be obligated to pay the Fair Market Value for any such Membership Units, without any discount for lack of marketability or minority ownership, unless the Class A Members unanimously agree otherwise.

4. Each Member that is a holder of Membership Units in the Company shall be entitled to have a certificate, signed by the Managers of the Company, exhibiting the number of Membership Units in the Company owned by such Member. All certificates representing

Membership Units which are subject to restrictions on transfer or to other restrictions may have imprinted thereon such notation to such effect as may be determined by the Managers.

5. No Member shall be required to make any Capital Contribution to the Company beyond the amounts set forth in this Article VI, except as may be agreed to by such Member in writing.

6. No interest shall accrue or be payable to any Member by reason of such Member's Capital Contribution or such Member's Capital Account.

7. Notwithstanding any inferences to the contrary in this Agreement, no Member (in such Member's capacity as a member) shall be personally liable for losses, costs, expenses, liabilities or obligations of the Company, nor shall any Manager be personally liable for losses, costs, expenses, liabilities or obligations of the Company.

8. The foregoing provisions of this Article VI are not intended to be for the benefit of any creditor or other person or entity (other than a Member in his or her capacity as a member of the Company) to whom or which any debts, liabilities or obligations are owed by (or who or which otherwise has any claim against) the Company or any of the Members; and no such creditor or other person or entity shall obtain any right under any of the foregoing provisions against the Company or any of the Managers or Members by reason of any debt, liability or obligation (or otherwise).

ARTICLE VII

Allocation of Profit and Loss

1. "Profit" and "Loss" shall, for purposes of this Agreement, mean, for each fiscal year of the Company or other period, an amount equal to the Company's taxable income, gain, loss or deduction for such year or period, determined by the Company's certified public accountants in accordance with I.R.C. Section 703(a), with the following adjustments:

    (a) All income or gain of the Company that is exempt from Federal income tax and not otherwise taken into account in computing

Profit and Loss pursuant to this Article VII-1 shall be added to such taxable income, gain, loss or deduction.

(b) Any expenditure of the Company described in I.R.C. Section 705(a)(2)(B) or treated as an expenditure described in such Section and not otherwise taken into account in computing Profit and Loss pursuant to this Article VII shall be subtracted from such taxable income, gain, loss or deduction.

2. Subject to the provisions of Article VII-3 hereof, the distributive shares of each item of Profit and Loss (or, if necessary, items thereof) for any Company Accounting Year or other period shall be allocated to each Member, to the extent of and in proportion to the amounts necessary to cause the respective Capital Account of each Member to be equal to the aggregate amount of distributions that each such Member would then have received if the Company's remaining capital at such time were distributed in accordance with Article XV-2 hereof.

3. The Company, with the review and concurrence of the Company's certified public accountants, shall allocate taxable income, gain, loss, credit, deduction (or items thereof) arising in any Company Accounting Year in a manner other than as provided in Article VII-2 hereof if, and to the extent that, the allocations otherwise provided under this Article VII would not be permissible under I.R.C. Sections 704(b) and/or 704(c). Any allocation made pursuant to and in accordance with this Article VII-3 shall be deemed to be a complete substitute for the allocation otherwise provided in Article VII-2 hereof, and no amendment of this Agreement shall be required with respect thereto, and each Member shall, for all purposes and in all respects, be deemed to have approved any such reasonable allocation, unless such allocation under this Article VII-3 would, or could, have a materially adverse effect on the balance of each Member's Capital Account relative to the balance of each Member's Capital Account had the allocation been made as provided for under Article VII-2 hereof.

4. If a Company Interest is transferred or assigned during a Company Accounting Year, that part of any item of Profit, Loss, income, gain, deduction, credit or basis allocated pursuant to this Article VII with respect to the Company Interest so transferred shall, in the reasonable

discretion of the Managers, either (i) be based on segmentization of the Company Accounting Year between the transferor and the transferee or (ii) be allocated between the transferor and the transferee in proportion to the number of days in such Company Accounting Year during which each owned such Company Interest, as disclosed by the Company's books and records.

ARTICLE VIII

Withdrawal of Member

1. In furtherance of the provisions of the Act, and except as otherwise set forth herein, no Member shall have the right, power or authority to withdraw from the Company or to demand and receive property of the Company or any distribution in return for such Member's Capital Contribution or Capital Account, prior to the dissolution and winding up of the Company.

2. Except as otherwise may be permitted under Articles XIII, XIV and XVI hereof, in the event that any Member withdraws from the Company in breach of this Agreement (including specifically, the provisions of Article VIII-1 above), such withdrawal shall, *ipso facto*, without any further action by the Company, the Managers or any other Members, constitute a default by the withdrawing Member under this Agreement, for which the Company and the other Members shall have all of their rights and remedies, at law or in equity, under this Agreement or under applicable law, including, without limitation, the right to recover damages, including, without limitation, reasonable attorneys' and paralegals' fees, from such withdrawing Member, which damages may offset the amount otherwise distributable to such withdrawing Member under the terms of this Agreement (including, without limitation, the provisions of Article XII hereof).

ARTICLE IX

Legal Title to Company Assets

1. Legal title to the Company Assets shall be held in the name of the Company or in any other manner which the Managers reasonably determine to be in the best interests of the Company.

2. It is expressly understood and agreed that the manner of holding title to the Company Assets is solely for the convenience of the Company. Accordingly, the spouse, heirs, executors or administrators, distributees, directors, officers, stockholders, members, managers, successors or assigns of any Member shall have no right, title or interest in or to any of the Company Assets by reason of the manner in which title is held; rather, the Company Assets shall be subject to the terms of this Agreement. It is further understood and agreed that the Members' Company Interest shall be considered personalty and not a real property interest; accordingly, the Members shall not have the right to demand or request a partition (or similar division) of any of the Company Assets.

ARTICLE X

Management; Indemnification

1. (a) Except as otherwise expressly provided in this Agreement, all management powers and decisions of the Company shall be exercised by or under the authority of, and the business and affairs of the Company shall be managed under the direction of, the Managers, who shall have all rights, powers and authority permitted by the laws of the State of Delaware as "managers" (as such term is defined and applied under the Act), and all decisions made for and on behalf of the Company by the Members shall be binding upon the Company. The Managers (acting for and on behalf of the Company), in extension and not in limitation of the rights and powers given them by law or by the other provisions of this Agreement, shall, in their reasonable discretion, have the full and entire right, power and authority, in the management of the Company business, to do any and all acts and things necessary, proper, convenient or advisable to effectuate the purposes of the Company, including, without limitation, negotiating the terms and conditions of contracts between the Company and the third party vendors, electing new Members, and establishing performance-based equity incentives for employees of the Company. The Managers shall devote to the management of the business of the Company such efforts and professional attention as reasonably necessary for the efficient operation of the Company business. Any

and all actions and/or decisions made for or on behalf of the Company by the Managers in accordance with the terms of this Agreement shall be made by a majority-in-number of the Managers and shall be binding upon the Company and the Members. In furtherance of the foregoing, any one of the Managers may execute documents and take other actions on behalf of the Company, which shall bind the Company when authorized by action of the Company pursuant to the provisions of this Agreement.

(b) In the event that there is an even number of Managers, any and all actions and/or decisions of such Managers with respect to the management and/or control of the Company and the Company business shall be taken or made jointly by such Managers, which actions and/or decisions shall be binding upon the Members and the Company. Notwithstanding the foregoing or anything to the contrary contained herein (including, without limitation, the provisions of Article XIX-3 hereof), in the event of a dispute, disagreement or deadlock between the Managers with respect to any material decision and/or action in connection with the management of the Company and the Company business, which the Managers are not able to resolve themselves after using their best efforts to do so (the "Disputed Issue"), then the Managers shall submit the Disputed Issue to binding arbitration, in which event the resolution of the Disputed Issue shall be made in accordance with the rules, regulations and procedures of the American Arbitration Association (as applicable in the State of Delaware). The resolution of any Disputed Issue by arbitration hereunder shall be final, binding and conclusive upon the Company, the Managers and the Members.

2. (a) Any Manager designated hereunder may resign at any time by giving written notice to the other Managers and the Members at least thirty (30) days prior to the effective date of such resignation; provided, however, that, notwithstanding the foregoing or anything to the contrary contained in this Agreement or under the Act, in no event shall any Manager designated hereunder be removed by the Members, unless such Manager engages in fraud or willful misconduct and the Members (other than a Member who is also

the Manager that engaged in such fraud or willful misconduct) unanimously agree and consent to such removal.

(b) In the event of the death, adjudication of insanity or incompetency, resignation or retirement (a "Withdrawal Event") of any Manager designated hereunder, the Members owning at least fifty-one percent (51%) of the total number of issued and outstanding Membership Units may appoint one (1) or more successor Managers, who shall have the right, power and authority to manage, oversee and administer the business and affairs of the Company in accordance with the provisions of this Agreement. No Person designated to serve as a Manager hereunder is required to be either a Member of the Company or a resident (or domestic corporation) of the State of Delaware.

3.   Notwithstanding anything to the contrary contained in this Agreement, the following is an exclusive list of major decisions that require the vote of a majority-in-Class A Units of the Class A Members entitled to vote. The Class A Members' authority and responsibility in voting on the following matters may not be delegated to any one or a group of Class A Members or officers or any committee established by the Managers:

(a) a sale of the Company (by way of merger, equity sale or asset sale, as the case may be);

(b) the hiring and compensation of any management-level employee at a rate of compensation that exceeds the annual compensation of the Company's Chief Executive Officer;

(c) effectuating an initial public offering of the Company's securities;

(d) liquidating, winding up or dissolving the Company; and

(e) commencing a formal bankruptcy proceeding involving the Company.

4.   (a) In furtherance of (but not in limitation of) the provisions of this Article X, the Members have the right, power and authority to designate one (1) or more persons (whether or not a Member) to serve

as executive Officers of the Company, including, without limitation, the designation of persons to serve as Chief Executive Officer, President, Vice President or Vice Presidents, Secretary, Treasurer and such other officers as the Members shall deem necessary or appropriate, who shall exercise such powers and perform such duties as shall from time to time be defined and determined by the Members, in their sole and absolute discretion. Any number of offices may be held by the same person. The Chief Executive Officer shall be responsible for supervision and direction of the day-to-day operations of the Company and shall report directly to, and be subject to the review and authority of, the Managers.

(b) Any Officer initially appointed hereunder or otherwise elected or appointed by the Members may be terminated and removed, with or without cause, at any time by the Members. Any vacancy occurring in any office of the Company may (but shall not be required to) be filled by the Members.

5. Unless otherwise provided herein, neither the Members nor any Officer shall be entitled to receive any payments, fees or other compensation for serving as a Member or Officer hereunder.

6. (a) [_____] is hereby designated the "Tax Matters Partner" (as such term is defined and used under the I.R.C. and the Treasury Regulations thereunder) of the Company.

(b) The Tax Matters Partner of the Company shall, within fifteen (15) business days of receipt thereof, forward to each Member a photocopy of any correspondence relating to the Company received from the Internal Revenue Service which relates to matters that are of material importance to the Company and/or its Members. The Tax Matters Partner of the Company shall, within fifteen (15) business days thereof, advise each Member in writing of the substance of any conversation held with any representative of the Internal Revenue Service which relates to matters that are of material importance to the Company and/or its Members.

(c) Any reasonable costs incurred by the Tax Matters Partner of the Company for retaining accountants, lawyers and/or other professionals on behalf of the Company in connection with dealing with the Internal Revenue Service on behalf of or with respect to the Company shall, upon the review of the Company's independent certified public accountants, be expenses of the Company; provided, however, that the Tax Matters Partner shall not incur any professional fees or expenses on behalf of the Company without the prior written approval of the Members.

7. In furtherance of the provisions of this Article X, the Managers may cause the Company to contract with any Person, including, without limitation, any of the Members, any entity in which any of the Members may have an interest and/or any Affiliated entity, at reasonable and competitive rates of compensation, commission or remuneration, for the performance of any and all services which may at any time be necessary, proper, convenient or advisable to carry on the business of the Company.

8. The Managers shall be fully and entirely reimbursed by the Company for any and all reasonable out-of-pocket costs and expenses incurred by the Managers in connection with the formation of the Company, the acquisition and transfer of the Company Assets and/or the management and supervision of the Company business; provided, however, that, with respect to any such reimbursement, the Managers shall present the Company with such invoices, in such detail and with such receipts, as are necessary to substantiate such out-of-pocket costs and expenses.

9. (a) The Managers and any authorized Officer (each an "Indemnified Party") shall be indemnified and held harmless by the Company from and against any and all claims, demands, liabilities, costs, expenses, damages and causes of action, of any nature whatsoever, arising out of or incidental to the management and supervision of the Company affairs, the acquisition of any Company Assets or as otherwise permitted under the Act, except where the claim at issue is based upon the gross negligence, fraud or willful misconduct of the Indemnified Party.

   (b) No Indemnified Party shall be liable, responsible or accountable in damages or otherwise to the Members or to the Company for any acts performed by such Indemnified Party in good faith and within the scope of this Agreement; provided, however, that, as noted in Article X-9(a) above, an Indemnified Party shall be liable for his actions and/or omissions to the extent the same are attributable to the gross negligence, fraud or willful misconduct of such Indemnified Party. No Indemnified Party shall be contractually liable under this Agreement or under the Act for the return of the Capital Account of any Member.

(c) The indemnification authorized by this Article X-9 shall include, but not be limited to, payment of (i) reasonable attorneys' and paralegals' fees or other expenses incurred in connection with settlement or in any finally adjudicated legal proceeding and (ii) the removal of any liens affecting any property of the indemnitee.

(d) The indemnification rights contained in this Article X-9 shall be cumulative of, and in addition to, any and all rights, remedies and recourses to which an Indemnified Party shall be entitled, whether pursuant to the provisions of this Agreement, at law or in equity. Indemnifications shall be made solely and entirely from the Company Assets, and no Member shall be personally liable to any indemnitee under this Article X-9. Furthermore, the provisions of this Article X-9 are not intended to be for the benefit of any creditor or other Person to whom or which any debts, liabilities or obligations are owed by (or who or which otherwise has a claim against) the indemnitee, and no such creditor or other Person shall obtain any right under the provisions of this Article X-9 against the Company or any Member by reason of any debt, liability or obligation of (or other claim against) the indemnitee.

ARTICLE XI

Bank Accounts; Books and Records; Tax Elections

1. The funds of the Company shall be deposited in such separate bank or investment account or accounts as shall be determined by the Managers, in their sole discretion, and the Managers shall arrange for the appropriate conduct of such account or accounts.

2. The books and records of the Company shall be kept, and the financial condition and the results of its operations recorded, in accordance with the accounting methods elected to be followed by the Company for Federal income tax purposes. The books and records of the Company shall reflect all Company transactions and shall be appropriate and adequate for the Company's business. The fiscal year of the Company for financial reporting and for Federal income tax purposes shall be the Company Accounting Year.

3. The Company shall keep at its principal office or at such other or additional offices (either within or without the State of Delaware) as the Managers shall deem advisable (a) books and records setting forth a current list of the full name and last known address of each Member, (b) a copy of the Certificate and this Agreement, and all amendments thereto, (c) copies of the Company's Federal, state and local income tax returns and personal property or intangible property tax returns, if any, for the three (3) most recent Company Accounting Years, (d) copies of any financial statements of the Company for the three (3) most recent Company Accounting Years, which reflect the Company's state of business and financial condition during such periods and (e) any other information and/or records required by the Act. Each Member (and such Member's duly authorized representative) shall have access to the books and records of the Company and the right to inspect and copy them, provided such request is reasonable and made at least five (5) business days in advance of such inspection, is done at reasonable hours and is done at such Member's personal expense.

4. If there is a distribution of the Company Assets (or any portion thereof) as described in I.R.C. Section 734, or if there is a transfer of any Company Interests as described in I.R.C. Section 743, then, upon the request of any Member, the Managers may (but shall not be required to) cause the Company to file an election under I.R.C. Section 754 to provide for an optional adjustment to the basis of Company Assets. Moreover, notwithstanding the possible future applicability of the provisions of I.R.C. Section 761(a), it is understood that no election shall be made by the Company or any Member to be excluded from the application of the provisions of Subtitle A, Chapter 1, Subchapter K of the I.R.C.

ARTICLE XII

Distributions

1. Notwithstanding anything to the contrary, the Managers (on behalf of the Company) shall, unless there are insufficient funds available, distribute to each Member at the conclusion of each Company Accounting Year (or within ninety (90) days thereafter), an amount equal to such Member's Tax Liability (provided that the Managers shall be under no obligation to cause the Company to borrow, lend or contribute to the Company the funds necessary to make such distributions).

2. Except to the extent Net Cash Flow shall be distributed upon termination of the Company pursuant to Article XV-2 hereof, all Net Cash Flow generated during a Company Accounting Year shall be distributed at such time or times as the Members may determine, in their reasonable discretion, during such Company Accounting Year in the following order of priority:

    (a) First, to the Class A Members, an amount equal to any respective accrued and unpaid Preferred Return;(b) Second to the Class A Members, aggregate amounts equal to any respective Additional Capital Contributions (if any);

    (b) Third, to the Class A Members, aggregate amounts equal to any respective Net Capital Investment; and

    (c) Finally, any and all remaining Net Cash Flow shall be distributed to the Members, *pro rata*, in proportion to their respective number of Membership Units in relation to the total number of issued and outstanding Membership Units.

3. All distributions made within the Company Accounting Year shall be subject to adjustment by reference to the financial statements for such Company Accounting Year. If any additional amount is to be distributed by reason of such financial statements, such additional amount shall be deemed a distribution for such Company Accounting Year; and if any excess amount was distributed during such Company Accounting Year, as

reflected by such financial statements, the excess amount shall be taken into account in reducing subsequent distributions.

ARTICLE XIII

Assignability of Company Interests

1. (a) Subject to the provisions of Articles XIII-2, XIV and XVI hereof, no Member shall sell, assign, transfer, convey, pledge, encumber, or in any way alienate or dispose of all or any portion of such Member's Company Interest, without delivering to the other Members a notice setting forth the terms and conditions of the proposed transfer and obtaining the prior written consent of the Managers (which consent shall be sole and absolute); provided, however, that such prior written consent shall not be required with respect to any transfers by a Member of all or any part of his, her or its Company Interest to any Permitted Transferee. Notwithstanding anything to the contrary contained in this Agreement, an assignee of a Member (including, without limitation, any Permitted Transferee) shall not become a Substituted Member unless: (x) the assigning Member so provides in the instrument of assignment, (y) the assignee agrees in writing to be bound by the provisions of this Agreement, and (z) the assigning Member, the Managers, the assignee and any other required signatory parties execute an amendment to this Agreement, which shall reflect, among other things, the admission of the assignee as a Substituted Member and the withdrawal of the assigning Member from the Company. Notwithstanding the foregoing, no such transfer to a Permitted Transferee or any other sale, transfer, conveyance, pledge or encumbrance will be permitted if such event would result in a violation of any applicable securities laws, as determined by the Managers.

(b) Notwithstanding the provisions of Article XIII-1(a) hereof, but subject to the provisions of Article XIII-2 hereof, in the event that a Member desires to sell, assign, transfer, convey, pledge, encumber, or in any way alienate all or any portion of his, her or its Company Interest, such Member must first give to the other Members (the "Offeree Members") notice of his, her or its intention to make such disposition, which notice shall specify the purchase price and payment terms (including collateral to secure the payment of any deferred payments) upon which the Offeror Member is willing to sell his, her or its Company Interest (the "Offer"). For a period of thirty (30) days from the receipt of such notice (the "Election Period"), the Offeree Members, *pro rata*, in proportion to the respective number of Membership Units owned by the Offeree Members in relation to the total number of issued and outstanding Membership Units (unless they agree upon another proportion), shall have the option (but not the obligation) to elect to purchase the Offering Member's Company Interest (or portion thereof) at the same price and upon the same terms and conditions as are set forth in the Offer. The Offer shall be in effect and irrevocable for the entire Election Period, during which the Offeror Member shall be prohibited from selling or otherwise disposing of his, her or its Company Interest (or portion thereof). If the Offeree Members (or any of them) choose(s) to accept the Offer, such Offeree Member(s) shall so notify the Offeror Member within the Election Period and closing shall take place at a mutually agreed time, place and date not later than ninety (90) days after such election. If such notice has not been given by the Offeree Member(s) prior to the expiration of the Election Period, or if the Offeree Member(s) do(es) not agree to purchase the Offeror Member's Company Interest (or portion thereof), the Offeror Member shall be free to dispose of his, her or its Company Interest to a third party, who or which is not Affiliated with the Offeror Member and is financially capable of carrying out the terms and conditions of the sale; provided, however, that any such disposition shall be made within one hundred twenty (120) days after the expiration of the Election Period; and provided, further, that such disposition shall be made for a purchase price no less than that contained in the Offer and on other terms and conditions at least as favorable to the Offeror Member as those contained in the Offer. In the event that the Offeror Member's Company Interest is not so disposed of within said one hundred twenty (120)-day period, the provisions of this Article XIII-1(b) shall again be applicable and must be complied with.

2. Notwithstanding anything contained in this Agreement to the contrary, it is expressly understood and agreed that no transfer of any Company Interests shall be made if such transfer would, or could, (i) jeopardize the partnership tax status of the Company for Federal and state income tax purposes or otherwise cause the Company to be treated as a publicly-traded partnership for Federal income tax purposes, (ii) result in a termination of the Company within the meaning of I.R.C. Section 708(b) unless all Members consent in writing to such transfer or substitution, or (iii) violate or cause the Company to violate, any state or Federal securities law or any other applicable law or governmental rule or regulation.

3. Notwithstanding anything to the contrary contained in this Agreement, the Managers shall not have the right to admit additional Members to the Company without the prior unanimous consent of the Members. Any authorized admission of additional Members under this Article XIII-4 (in contrast to an assignment of an existing Company Interest under Article XIII-1 hereof) shall dilute, *pro rata*, all Company Interests of the Members existing at the time of such admission.

4. Unless named in this Agreement or otherwise admitted to the Company in accordance with the terms of this Agreement, no Person shall be considered a Member. The Company, the Managers, each Member and any other Persons having business with the Company need deal only with Members so named or so admitted; they shall not be required to deal with any other Person by reason of an assignment by a Member or by reason of the termination of a Member, except as otherwise provided in this Agreement. In the absence of the substitution of a Member for an assigning or terminated Member, any payment to a Member or to his, her or its legal representatives shall acquit the Company, the Managers and the Members of all liability to any other Person(s) who or which may be interested in such payment by reason of an assignment by, or the termination of, such Member.

ARTICLE XIV

Bankruptcy of a Member

In the event of the Bankruptcy of a Member (the "Bankrupt Member"), the other Members (the "Continuing Members"), in accordance with their respective number of Membership Units in relation to the total number of issued and outstanding Membership Units (unless they agree upon another proportion), shall have the option (but not the obligation), exercisable by giving notice thereof to the Bankrupt Member or to such Bankrupt Member's trustee in Bankruptcy, guardian, receiver or other legal representative, to purchase all (but not less than all) of the Bankrupt Member's Company Interest, within ninety (90) days after the event of such Bankruptcy, at a price equal to the Fair Market Value of such Company Interest as determined in accordance with Article I hereof. Within sixty (60) days after the joint written report required to determine the Fair Market Value of such Bankrupt Member's Company Interest or written report of the third (3rd) appraiser (as the case may be) has been rendered, the Continuing Members shall give notice to the legal representative of the Bankrupt Member of their decision as to the exercise of the aforesaid option. If such option is exercised, settlement shall be held within thirty (30) days from the date of such exercise. The terms of payment shall be all cash or as otherwise agreed upon by the respective parties.

ARTICLE XV

Dissolution and Termination of Company

1. The Company shall be dissolved, the Company Assets shall be disposed of, and its affairs wound up, upon the earliest to occur of the following events:

    (a) the prior written unanimous consent of the Managers, subject to Article X-3(d) hereof; or

    (b) at any time the Company has no Members for a period of ninety (90) consecutive days; or

    (c) the entry of a decree of judicial dissolution under §18-802 of the Act.

    Notwithstanding the foregoing or anything to the contrary contained in this Agreement and in furtherance of §18-801(a)(4) of the Act, the death, resignation, retirement, expulsion, termination or Bankruptcy of a Member, or other event of dissociation of a Member from the Company shall not constitute an event of dissolution of the Company.

2. The Company shall terminate when all the Company Assets have been disposed of (except for any liquid assets not so disposed of), and the net proceeds therefrom, as well as any other liquid or illiquid assets of the Company, shall, unless otherwise required by the Act, be distributed as follows: (i) first, to the creditors of the Company for the payment or due provisions for the liabilities of the Company (including loans, if any, to the Company from Members), and (ii) second, to the Class A Members and Class B Members, *pro rata*, in accordance with their respective positive Capital Account balances (after the allocation of all items of Profit, Loss, deduction, credit and deduction (or items thereof) under and pursuant to Article VII hereof).

3. Following the distribution of the net proceeds under Article XV-2 hereof and the completion of winding up the affairs of the Company, any Member, is hereby authorized and directed to have prepared and file a certificate of cancellation of the Company with the Office of the Secretary of State of Delaware, in accordance with §18-203 of the Act, and take any and all other actions as may be necessary and/or appropriate under the Act to dissolve and terminate the Company.

ARTICLE XVI

Termination of Employment of a Member

1. (a) Notwithstanding anything to the contrary contained in this Agreement, including, specifically, but without limitation, the provisions of Article XIII-1 hereof, in the event that a Class B Member's employment terminates for any reason other than a termination by the Company for Cause (as defined below), the Company shall redeem and liquidate all of the Class B Membership Units owned by such Member (hereinafter referred to as "Terminated Member") for a redemption amount equal to the following:

    (i) if the terminating event occurs on or after the first (1st) anniversary of a Class B Member's starting date with the Company (the "First Anniversary Date"), but before the end of the first fiscal quarter thereafter, twenty-five percent (25%) of the Fair Market Value of the Terminating Member's Class B Membership Units as of the date of such terminating event; and

(ii) an additional six and one quarter percent (6.25%) of the Fair Market Value of the Terminating Member's Class B Membership Units for each complete fiscal quarter following the First Anniversary Date that the Class B Member shall have been employed with the Company as of the date of the terminating event; provided, however, that no Class B Member shall be entitled to a redemption amount exceeding one hundred percent (100%) of the Fair Market Value of the Terminating Member's Class B Membership Units. As an example, if the terminating event occurs immediately after the start of the second quarter after the third (3rd) anniversary of a Terminated Member's starting date, the Company shall redeem and liquidate all of the Class B Membership Units owned by such Terminated Member for a redemption amount equal to eighty-one and one quarter percent (81.25%) of the Fair Market Value of the Terminating Member's Class B Membership Units as of the date of such terminating event (25% + (9 x 6.25%) = 81.25%).

(b) Notwithstanding anything to the contrary contained in this Agreement, if any time during the term of existence of the Company, the Terminating Member later participates, directly or indirectly, as an employee, consultant, independent contractor, officer, manager, owner, investor, director, stockholder, member, partner or otherwise have a financial interest in a Competing Business, then the payment terms of the redemption amount due to the Terminating Member shall be those set forth in Article XVI-2 and the Company shall have the right to offset any future payments of the redemption amount against any amounts still payable to the Terminating Member.

2. (a) In the event that a Class B Member's employment is terminated for Cause, the Company shall redeem and liquidate all of the Class B Membership Units owned by such Terminated Member for a redemption amount equal to fifty percent (50%) of the amount that such Terminated Member otherwise would have received pursuant to Article XVI-1 hereof. For purposes of this Article XVI, "Cause" means a termination of employment due to any of the following: (i)

commission of a willful act of dishonesty in the course of such Member's duties hereunder, which is reasonably likely to cause material injury to the Corporation, (ii) conviction of such Member by a court of competent jurisdiction or a *nolo contendere* plea with respect to a crime constituting a felony, or conviction or a *nolo contendere* plea in respect of any act involving fraud, dishonesty or moral turpitude, (iii) performance by such Member under the influence of non-prescription controlled substances, or continued habitual intoxication, during working hours, (iv) material non-compliance with any of the policies and procedures of the Company, or (v) any breach of any material contractual obligations with the Company as set forth in any document including, without limitation, any employment agreement or binding offer letters by and between the Company and any employee of the Company.

(b) In the event that a Class B Member's employment is terminated for any reason other than for Cause, the Company shall have the option to redeem any and all Class B Units owned by such Class B Member for the Fair Market Value of any Company Interest redeemed pursuant to this Article XVI-2(b), subject to any restrictions placed on such Class B Units as set forth in Article XVI-1 hereof; it being understood and agreed that the determination to redeem any Class B Units pursuant to this Article XVI-2(b) shall be made in the sole and absolute discretion of the Managers.

3. In the event that a Class A Member's employment is terminated for Cause, the Company shall have the option to redeem any and all Class A Units owned by such Class A Member for the Fair Market Value of any Company Interest redeemed pursuant to this Article XVI-3; it being understood and agreed that the determination to redeem any Class A Units pursuant to this Article XVI-3 shall be made in the sole and absolute discretion of the Managers.

4. Settlement on the redemption and liquidation of the Company Interests owned by the Terminated Member under this Article XVI shall be held at the principal office of the Company within ninety (90) days following a terminating event. At settlement on a redemption of the Company Interests owned by the Terminated Member under this Article XVI, the

Terminated Member (or his or her personal representatives) shall execute and deliver (or cause to be executed and delivered) to the Company an amendment to this Agreement and any other documents, instruments and agreements that the Company determines are necessary and/or appropriate to reflect, among other things, the complete redemption and liquidation by the Company of the Company Interests owned by the Terminated Member, the withdrawal of the Terminated Member (and, if applicable, any other owner of the Company Interests owned by the Terminated Member) as a Member and, if applicable, the resignation of the Terminated Member as an Officer of the Company, and the Company shall pay to the Terminated Member twenty percent (20%) of the Redemption Amount in immediately available funds and, with respect to the remaining eighty percent (80%), the Company shall execute and deliver to the Terminated Member a promissory note representing the balance of the purchase price payable in five (5) equal annual installments, together with accrued interest computed at an interest rate equal to the mid-term Applicable Federal Rate pursuant to Section 1274(d) of the I.R.C. in effect as of the date of such promissory note, beginning on the first (1st) anniversary of the date of settlement hereunder.

5. In the event that the Company is sold (by way of merger, equity sale or asset sale, as the case may be), the Managers of the Company shall have the sole discretion to remove any restrictions, as set forth in Article XVI-1 hereof, placed on any or all of the Class B Membership Units and the Company shall have the option to redeem any and all of the Class B Membership Units for the Fair Market Value of such Class B Member's Company Interest represented by the number of Class B Membership Units redeemed pursuant to this Article XVI-5.

6. Notwithstanding the provisions set forth in Article XVI hereof, the Managers of the Company may, in their sole and absolute discretion, waive any restrictions, as set forth in Article XVI hereof or otherwise, placed on any or all of the Class B Membership Units granted to non-employees of the Company.

7. (a) If at any time a non-employee Class B Member ("Offered Non-Employee Member") receives a bona fide offer to purchase any or all

of such Offered Non-Employee Member's Class B Membership Units (a "Third Party Offer") from a third party (an "Offeror"), which the Offered Non-Employee Member wishes to accept, the Offered Non-Employee Member shall cause the Third Party Offer to be reduced to writing and shall notify the Company in writing of its wish to accept the Third Party Offer. The Offered Non-Employee Member's notice to the Company shall contain an irrevocable offer to sell such Class B Membership Units to the Company (in the manner set forth below), and shall be accompanied by a copy of the Third Party Offer (which shall identify the Offeror). At any time within thirty (30) days after the date of the receipt by the Company of the Offered Non-Employee Member's notice, the Company shall have the right to elect, by delivery of notice to the Offered Non-Employee Member (an "Election Notice"), to redeem all or any portion of the Class B Membership Units covered by the Third Party Offer at the same price and on the same terms and conditions as the Third Party Offer (or, if the Third Party Offer includes any consideration other than cash, then at the sole option of the Company, at the equivalent all-cash price, determined in good faith by the Managers).

(b) The closing of any redemption, pursuant to Article XVI-7(a) hereof, shall occur within forty-five (45) days of delivery by the Company of its Election Notice (or such later time as is necessary to satisfy or obtain any regulatory approval) to the Offered Non-Employee Member. At the closing, the Company shall deliver a check or checks in the appropriate amount (or by wire transfer of immediately available funds, if the Offered Non-Employee Member provides to the Company wire transfer instructions) (and any such non-cash consideration to be paid) to the Offered Non-Employee Member against any instruments, if any, representing the Class B Membership Units so redeemed, appropriately endorsed by the Offered Non-Employee Member.

(c) If at the end of the thirty (30) day period referred to in Article XVI-7(a) hereof, the Company has not tendered an Election Notice to the Offered Non-Employee Member in the manner set forth above, the Offered Member may, during the succeeding sixty

(60) day period, sell not less than all of the Class B Membership Units covered by the Third Party Offer, to the Offeror on terms no less favorable to the Offered Non-Employee Member than those contained in the Third Party Offer. Promptly after such sale, the Offered Non-Employee Member shall notify the Company of the consummation thereof and shall furnish such evidence of the completion and time of completion of such sale and of the terms thereof as may reasonably be requested by the Company. If, at the end of the sixty (60) day period referred to above, the Offered Non-Employee Member has not completed the sale of such Class B Membership Units as aforesaid, any and all of the restrictions on sale, transfer or assignment contained in this Agreement shall again be in effect with respect to such Class B Membership Units.

ARTICLE XVII

Confidentiality Provisions and Covenants Against Competition and Solicitation

1. Except as otherwise expressly permitted in writing by the Company, no Member (for purposes of this Article XVII, the term "Member" shall include any member, manager, partner, stockholder, officer or director of a Member hereof and, in the event that an entity is the Member shall:

(a) use the Proprietary Information for any purpose other than the purpose for which the Company shared such information with such Member; or

(b) directly or indirectly copy, transfer, or otherwise disclose or reveal Proprietary Information to any person or entity other than the partners, employees, directors, officers, agents and consultants or a Member or Affiliate thereof who (i) have a need to know in connection with the relationship and/or discussions of the parties hereto, (ii) have been advised of such Proprietary Information's confidential status and (iii) are subject to legally binding obligations of confidentiality as to such Proprietary Information that are no less restrictive than those contained in this Agreement.

2. Each Member shall use at least the same degree (but no less than a reasonable degree) of care and protection to prevent the unauthorized use, dissemination or copying of any Proprietary Information as such Member uses to protect his, her or its own information of a like nature.

3. Each Member agrees not to assert any claim of title or ownership to the Proprietary Information or any portion thereof. If Proprietary Information consists of computer software disclosed in object code form, such Member shall not, and shall not permit any other party, to reverse engineer, reverse compile, or disassemble such object code, or take any other steps to derive a source code equivalent thereof.

4. If a Member becomes legally compelled (by depositions, interrogatory, subpoena, civil investigative demand or similar process) to disclose any Proprietary Information, he or she agrees to provide the Company with prompt prior written notice of such requirement so that the Company may seek a protective order or other appropriate remedy. If such protective order or other remedy is not obtained, or if the Company waives, in writing, compliance with the terms hereof, such Member agrees to furnish only that portion of the Proprietary Information which he is advised by written opinion of his, her or its counsel is legally required, and to exercise reasonable efforts to obtain confidential treatment of such information.

5. Each Member hereby agrees that he or she shall destroy or return to the Company all copies of Proprietary Information promptly upon the earlier of (a) the Company's request at any time or (b) the termination of the membership in the Company of such Member.

6. During the period of time that a Member is a member of the Company and for two (2) years after such Member ceases to be a member, such Member shall not, with respect to the businesses described in Article XVII-7 hereof, directly or indirectly, whether as a proprietor, member, partner, stockholder, officer, consultant, independent contractor, co-venturer, employer, employee, agent, representative or in any other capacity, solicit business from, divert business from or perform services to or for any customer, client or account of the Company, including any customer, client or account over which such Member had responsibility or significant contact.

7. During the period of time that a Member is a member of the Company and for two (2) years after such Member ceases to be a member, such Member shall not engage, directly or indirectly, in any Competing Business, whether as a proprietor, member, partner, stockholder, officer, consultant, independent contractor, co-venturer, employer, employee, agent, representative or in any other capacity, in any country or political subdivision in which the Company or any Affiliate conducts business or in any country or political subdivision of the world in which the Company or any Affiliate has, within the immediately preceding twelve (12) months, expressed an intention to conduct business.

8. During the period of time that a Member is a member of the Company and for two (2) years after such Member ceases to be a member, such Member shall not directly or indirectly, whether as a proprietor, member, partner, stockholder, officer, consultant, independent contractor, co-venturer, employer, employee, agent, representative or in any other capacity, employ, recruit, solicit for employment, or for the purposes of hiring or engaging, any employee of the Company or any individual who was employed by the Company during the previous one (1)-year period.

9. If a Member shall violate any of the covenants or agreements under this Article XVII, the Company shall be entitled to an accounting and repayment of all gross profits, compensation, commissions, remunerations or benefits which such Member directly or indirectly realized and/or may realize as a result of, growing out of or in connection with any such violation; such remedy shall be in addition to and not in limitation of any injunctive relief or other rights or remedies to which the Company is or may be entitled at law or in equity or under this Agreement. The Company shall also be entitled to recover all costs and expenses, including, without limitation, reasonable fees of attorneys and paralegals that are incurred as a result of, growing out of or in connection with any such violation. Each party consents to personal jurisdiction in any such action brought in the State of Delaware and waives any objection or defense that such jurisdiction is invalid.

10. Each Member acknowledges that his, her or its agreement not to disclose Proprietary Information, as provided herein, is made as an inducement to the other parties hereto, to enter into this Agreement.

Each Member and the Company have carefully read and considered the provisions of this Article XVII and, having done so, agree that the restrictions set forth in such sections are fair and reasonable and are reasonably required for the protection of the interests of the Company, any Affiliate, and the respective members, partners, stockholders, officers, directors and employees of the same.

11. Each Member shall disclose promptly to the Company and any Affiliate any and all significant conceptions and ideas for inventions, improvements, and valuable discoveries, whether patentable or not, that are conceived or made by such Member, solely or jointly with another, as a result of his, her or its exposure to Proprietary Information or his, her or its membership in, or management of, the Company, and that the Company views as directly related to the business or activities of the Company or any Affiliate, regardless of whether or not such ideas, inventions or improvements qualify as "works for hire." Each Member hereby assigns and agrees to assign all his, her or its interests in such ideas, inventions or improvements to the Company. Whenever requested to do so by the Company, such Member shall execute any and all applications, assignments or other instruments that the Company shall deem necessary to apply for and obtain Letters Patent of the United States or any foreign country or to otherwise protect the Company's interest therein.

12. Each Member shall disclose promptly to the Company and any Affiliate any and all significant works, and any and all derivative works thereof, that are created by such Member as a result of his, her or its exposure to Proprietary Information or his, her or its membership in, or management of, the Company, solely or jointly with another, and that the Company reasonably views as directly related to the business or activities of the Company or any Affiliate, regardless of whether such works qualify as "works for hire." Each Member hereby assigns and agrees to assign all his, her or its interests in such works to the Company. Whenever requested to do so by the Company, each Member shall take all actions and cooperate as is necessary to protect the copyrightability of the works and further agrees to execute any documents that might be necessary to perfect the Company's ownership of copyrights in such works including registration thereof.

13. If any provision or part of any provision of this Agreement shall for any reason be held invalid, illegal or unenforceable in any respect, the remaining provisions and remaining parts of provisions, as the case may be, shall be construed as if such invalid, illegal or unenforceable provision or part of a provision had never been contained herein. Further, in the event that a court declares that the imposition of a time period and/or an area of restriction is reasonable or needs to be adjusted for purposes of the enforceability of this Agreement, then this Agreement shall be appropriately modified so that such time period and/or area of restriction shall be deemed to be part of this Agreement.

ARTICLE XVIII

Miscellaneous Provisions

1. The Members hereby agree to execute and deliver all documents (subject to the provisions of Article XVII-5), provide all information and take or refrain from all such action as may be reasonably necessary or appropriate to achieve the purposes of this Agreement and the Certificate.

2. Except as expressly provided in this Agreement, nothing contained herein shall be construed to constitute any Member the agent of any other Member hereof or to limit in any manner the Members in the carrying on of their own respective businesses or activities. Each Member may engage in and/or possess any interest in other business ventures of every nature and description, independently or with others, whether existing as of the date hereof or hereafter coming into existence; and neither the Company nor any Member hereof shall have any rights in or to any such independent ventures or the income or profits derived therefrom.

3. Unless otherwise provided herein, the Managers and Members hereby agree that, in connection with any dispute between or among the Managers and/or the Members with respect to any decision to be made or action to be taken, the parties shall, for thirty (30) days from the date such dispute arises, use good faith efforts to resolve such dispute in the best interests of the Company. In furtherance of the foregoing, it is understood and agreed by and among the parties hereto that, upon the

expiration of such thirty (30)-day period, any such claim or controversy shall, upon the request of any party (or parties) involved, be submitted to and settled by non-binding mediation. In the event that the parties fail to resolve such claim or controversy through non-binding mediation and as a condition precedent to any litigation with respect to any claim or controversy arising out of or relating to this Agreement (or a breach hereof) and/or the Company, then the parties shall submit the claim or controversy to binding arbitration, in which event the resolution of the claim or controversy shall be made in accordance with the rules, regulations and procedures of the American Arbitration Association (as applicable in the State of Delaware). The resolution of any claim or controversy by binding arbitration hereunder shall be final, binding and conclusive upon the Company, the Managers and the Members.

4. (a) All notices provided for herein shall be in writing, hand-delivered, with receipt therefor, or sent by certified or registered mail, return receipt requested, and first-class postage prepaid, or by overnight courier, to the address of each Member as shown in Exhibit A, unless notice of a change of address is given to the Company pursuant to the provisions of this Article XVIII-4. Any notice which is required to be given within a stated period of time shall be considered timely if delivered or postmarked before midnight of the last day of such period. Any notice made hereunder shall be deemed effective for all purposes and in all respects when sent (or given) to any Member at the address set forth in Exhibit A hereof, or at such other address specified by a Member for which notice has been received by the Company in accordance with this Article XVIII-4.

   (b) Where the consent or approval of any Member is required by this Agreement, the failure of such Member to respond (either affirmatively or negatively) in writing after the Company has sent two (2) notices requesting such approval to such Member, with the second such notice being sent by the Company at least ten (10) days following the first such notice, then, after the expiration of ten (10) days following the date the second such notice was sent, such failure to respond shall be conclusively deemed the affirmative consent or approval of such Member.

5. Any and all amendments to this Agreement shall require the affirmative vote of the majority-in-Membership Units of the Class A Members; *provided, however,* that any and all amendments to this Agreement that will adversely affect any substantive right of a Class A Member shall require the unanimous vote of the Membership Units of the Class A Members.

6. By executing this Agreement, each Member (who is not otherwise a Manager) irrevocably makes, constitutes and appoints the Managers as such Member's true and lawful attorney-in-fact and agent with full power and authority in his, her or its name, place and stead to make, execute, sign, acknowledge, deliver, file and record with respect to the Company the following:

    (a) All amendments to this Agreement and/or the Certificate and all other instruments and documents which the Managers deem appropriate to qualify or to continue the Company as a limited liability company in each jurisdiction in which the Company conducts business;

    (b) All instruments which the Managers deem appropriate to reflect (i) any change or modification of the terms and conditions governing the relationship among the Members and the Company or (ii) an amendment of this Agreement and/or the Certificate, made in accordance with this Agreement;

    (c) All conveyances and other instruments, certificates or documents which the Managers deem appropriate to effect, evidence and/or reflect any sales or transfers by, or the dissolution, termination and/or liquidation of, the Company, including any sales or transfer of Company Interests pursuant to this Agreement;

    (d) All such other instruments, documents and certificates which may from time to time be required by the Company, its lenders, the Internal Revenue Service, the State of Delaware, the United States of America, or any political subdivision within which the Company conducts its business, to effectuate, implement, continue and defend the valid and continuing existence of the Company as a limited liability company and to carry out the intention and purpose of this Agreement; and

(e) All amendments to this Agreement and any other documents, instruments and certificates which may be required to admit additional Members or Substituted Members. If a Member assigns its Company Interest under and pursuant to Article XIII or XIV hereof, the foregoing power of attorney shall survive the delivery of the instruments effecting such assignment for the purpose of enabling the Managers to sign, swear to, execute, acknowledge and file any amendments to the Certificate and other instruments and documents in order to effectuate the substitution of the assignee as a Member. It is expressly intended that the foregoing power of attorney under this Article XVIII-5 is a durable power of attorney which shall not be affected by the subsequent physical or mental disability or incapacity of a Member, and such power of attorney is coupled with an interest; provided, however, that the Managers shall not exercise the same in any manner which would (i) remove a Manager, (ii) enlarge any obligation or liability of a Member, or (iii) affect any Company distributions in a manner materially adverse to any Member, except to the extent any Member adversely affected thereby has previously consented thereto in writing.

7. This Agreement and the rights of the parties hereunder will be governed by, interpreted and enforced in accordance with the laws of the State of Delaware, without regard to principles of conflicts of laws or choice of law.

8. This Agreement shall inure to the benefit of and bind the parties hereto, and their respective members, managers, partners, legal representatives, successors and, subject to the provisions of Article XIII hereof, assigns.

9. This Agreement, together with Exhibit A attached hereto, and the Certificate set forth and are intended by all parties hereto to be an integration of all of the promises, agreements, conditions, understandings, warranties and representations between the parties hereto with respect to the Company, the Company's business and the Company Assets, and there are no promises, agreements, conditions, understandings, warranties or representations, oral or written, express or implied, except as set forth herein.

10. If any provision of this Agreement is held to be illegal, invalid or unenforceable under the present or future laws effective during the

term of this Agreement, such provision will be fully severable; this Agreement will be construed and enforced as if such illegal, invalid or unenforceable provision had never comprised a part of this Agreement; and the remaining provisions of this Agreement will remain in full force and effect and will not be affected by the illegal, invalid or unenforceable provision or by its severance from this Agreement.

11. This Agreement is made solely and specifically among and for the benefit of the parties hereto, and their respective successors and assigns, subject to the express provisions hereof relating to successors and assigns, and no other Person will have any rights, interest or claims hereunder or be entitled to any benefits under or on account of this Agreement as a third party beneficiary or otherwise. In furtherance of and not in limitation of the foregoing, nothing contained in this Agreement is intended to be for the benefit of any creditor or other Person (other than a Member in his, her or its capacity as a member of the Company) to whom or which any debts, liabilities or obligations are owed by the Company or any of the Members; and no such creditor or other Person shall obtain any right hereunder against the Company or any of the Members by reason of any debt, liability or obligation (or otherwise).

12. This Agreement may be executed in several counterparts, each of which will be deemed an original but all of which together will constitute one and the same instrument.

{ Signatures appear on the following page. }

The undersigned parties have executed this Limited Liability Company
Agreement as of the date first above written.

WITNESS   **MEMBERS:**

[_____]

_____   By: _____
[_____]

_____   _____
[_____]

_____   _____
[_____]

EXHIBIT A
TO
LIMITED LIABILITY COMPANY AGREEMENT
OF
NEWCO, LLC

Class A Members:	**Capital Contributions**	**Percentage Company Interest**
[_____]	[_____]	[_____]
[_____]	[_____]	[_____]
[_____]	[_____]	[_____]
	_____	_____
Totals	[_____]	100.0%

Class B Members

None

ABOUT THE AUTHORS

Frank A. Ciatto helps entrepreneurs succeed in new business ventures. His legal knowledge and practical experience help ensure that owners and investors realize the full value of their ideas and investments. With nearly 20 years' experience launching new ventures, he focuses on mergers and acquisitions, limited liability companies, private equity investments, tax and accounting issues, corporate finance transactions, and succession planning.

Joseph B. Walker Jr. focuses on corporate transactional matters, including mergers and acquisitions, loan, financing, and other strategic transactions for a variety of clients in his practice. He represents business entities of all sizes, in various industries, in connection with corporate law and securities matters. He has experience in drafting, structuring, and negotiating a wide variety of transaction documents including merger agreements, licensing agreements, operating agreements, stock purchase agreements, real estate purchase agreements, commercial leases, and joint venture agreements.

ASPATORE